CATCHING IDLE BUTTERFLIES

Andra Marquardt

All scriptural references are from the New International Version (NIV), New Living Translation (NLT), English Standard Version (ESV), King James Version (KJV), and The Jewish Publication Society (JPS). Each version is noted with each scriptural passage throughout the book.

ISBN: 979-8-218-23947-3

Cover photo by Andra Marquardt

ACKNOWLEDGMENTS

No writing endeavor is ever completed in a vacuum.

I may have spent many sweat-and-tear-inducing hours typing the following words, but they wouldn't make much sense without the kind and thoughtful advice of the Wordsmiths who so graciously accepted me into their flock.

My constant gratitude goes to my husband, Dave, who never seems to mind all the hours when I'm figuratively glued to my computer.

To my son, Tom, who never ceases to bring me joy and laughter.

To you, Dear Reader, who took a chance on this nobody of a writer by picking up this book and reading the words therein.

And lastly, to Jesus who not only saved me (and continues to save me) but pushes me to keep writing when at times I would rather do anything else. Like the laundry.

TABLE OF CONTENTS

INTRODUCTION

For me, the most difficult part of writing a book is deciding on a title. How does one boil an entire book—no matter its length—down to a few words while at the same time convey what it's about? And in a way that'll attract readers?

I've kept a journal since I was a teenager, and I started a blog in 2006 which continues today.

The entries for this book fall into one of four categories (although you will find some overlap):

1. Life
2. Culture
3. Politics (fear not, this is the shortest one)
4. Faith

I once titled one of my blogs "Catching Idle Butterflies." As part of the introduction, I added a freestyle poem:

I am but a seeker of God's wisdom, knowledge, mercy, and strength,
a record of my ever-continuing journey.
Each is a butterfly,
sitting idle but for a moment,
so I might catch it,
learn,
grow,
and understand.

Followed by:

Tune your ears to wisdom,
and concentrate on understanding.
Cry out for insight,
and ask for understanding.
Search for them as you would for silver;
seek them like hidden treasures.
Then you will understand what it means to fear the Lord,

I figured that would be a fitting title for this book.
Those idle butterflies I managed to catch.

PART 1: LIFE

CONVERSATIONS WITH MINI-ME

(June 4, 2017)

For the longest time I didn't like me. I am silly and weird, and too often too smart for my own good. People teased me as a youngin', sometimes mercilessly. I soon believed that being silly and weird was wrong, and in order to be loved and accepted, I needed to be different. I needed to be "normal."

Whatever that is.

Only after I reached my 20s did I realize how much energy it took to be something I wasn't. It left me mentally and spiritually exhausted. Not only that, but people didn't accept me as much as I hoped they would.

Where did I go wrong? How can I be loved and accepted *and* be the person God meant me to be?

So I went on a little journey, and I talked to the little girl inside me. The one untouched by pain, the one who believed in herself and everything around her. A little girl filled with an immeasurable hope and certainty that nothing could ever go wrong.

It didn't take long for me to realize that's the person God wanted me to be—in all her silliness and weirdness. In all her hopefulness and innocence. Unscarred by time.

Now in the last half of my 40s, I've not only decided to embrace my weirdness and silliness, but the joy that comes from not acting like an adult all the time. It's okay to be childlike. To run around giggling. To make funny faces at people.

After all, if children know anything, they know how to embrace joy and express it with no regard how it may look to others. They study the world around them, not with boredom or cynicism, but with wonder and awe.

That's what my mini-me reminds me to do when I feel the pressure of impossible expectations.

It's okay to be silly. It's okay to be weird. After all, if everyone was "normal," how boring life would be.

Converse with and embrace your own inner child, in all his or her glorious silliness and weirdness. Those conversations may also help lead you to the person God meant you to be.

At that time the disciples came to Jesus and asked, "Who, then, is the greatest in the kingdom of heaven?"
He called a little child to him, and placed the child among them. And he said: "Truly I tell you, unless you change and become like little children, you will never enter the kingdom of heaven. Therefore, whoever takes the lowly position of this child is the greatest in the kingdom of heaven. And whoever welcomes one such child in my name welcomes me."
~Matthew 18:1-5 (NIV)

I WANT TO BE LIKE ME WHEN I GROW UP

(October 22, 2017)

The following touches upon the same subject as the previous one, but from a slightly different perspective.

I don't recall someone ever saying the above title. In fact, this is the first time I've strung those words in that order. I've always used someone else in place of "me," whether it's one of my parents, a famous person, or someone who chose to do something extraordinary or worthy of respect—perhaps even awe:

"I want to be as successful as that person someday."

"I want to be as kind and generous as that person someday."

"I want to write like that person someday."

I'll bet the people we admire, and who we believe have reached the pinnacle of "the perfect life" have said the same thing.

Mentors have their own mentors, and heroes have their own heroes.

Don't get me wrong. We need heroes, mentors, and leaders, because they inspire us to reach further toward our own dreams and goals. The downside of that, however, is inspiration can twist into envy and jealousy. We can pay so much attention to those we admire, we soon reach the realization that we will never be who they are.

I am me the same way you are you. No one can be me anymore than I can be them. We can have similar dreams and aspirations, but the similarity ends there. How I reach my goal will be far different from how you reach yours. Our successes and failures are as unique as our DNA.

What brought this thought about was reading something by an author I admire. His words seemed to flow off the page, and I thought, "Why can't I write like that? To have his wisdom and eloquence?"

As usual, God led me to his Word to convict me of my envy:

You made all the delicate, inner parts of my body
and knit me together in my mother's womb.
Thank you for making me so wonderfully complex!

~Psalm 139:13-18 (NLT)

God made me the way he did for many reasons, not just one. His gifts to me are for specific purposes that no one can steal, copy, or take over.

The reverse is also true. I can't steal, copy, or take over anyone else's gifts or life goals. Or their successes. I must always be cognizant of what inspires me and avoid the too-easy twist into envy. Doing so could destroy the dreams God made for me. In the end I fail at being me—the way God meant for me to be.

The same is true for you, so go out there and strive to be you when you grow up.

EYES WIDE OPEN

(January 23, 2018)

When it comes to photography, I always keep my eyes open for something interesting to photograph and share. I loved today especially, because it was cold, calm, and foggy. Hoarfrost abounded on the trees, grass, and shrubs.

What normally takes me fifteen minutes to walk around a few blocks during my breaks almost doubled today because I couldn't get enough of the frost-coated—everything.

Unfortunately, I too often don't have that kind of "eyes wide open" mentality toward my writing—or even my faith at times.

I ran into a quote the other day:

"If you wait for inspiration to write, you're not a writer, you're a waiter."

~ Dan Poynter.

I also found something I had written years ago to keep me motivated:

"Write fearless. Anything less, it shows, and the words inevitably stumble and fall."

Fear holds me back. Fear of offense, of being misunderstood, of boring my readers, my how the list is long!

Some people call writing—whether fiction or non-fiction—their ministry. They write to bring people closer to God. It's a calling like any other type of ministry.

I, on the other hand, don't. To me writing is my form of worship. Do I want to encourage people with my words? Absolutely. I'll even admit that I hope my words will bring others closer to God. To see his love and beauty as I do. I also believe writing is my calling, because as much as I may complain about quitting, I never will. I can't. God won't let me (and believe me, I've tried).

I hesitate to call it my ministry because I stumble so much. I don't know enough about Jesus, scripture, or faith in general to claim any kind of authority. To me, ministry as a form of spiritual leadership, and because I too often don't know what the heck I'm doing, I don't want anyone to follow me. I'll only make them stumble as much as I do, if not more.

That kind of thinking, however, limits God. If God wants me to reach others with my words, then I have to put those words out there and trust they will reach the right people at the right time.

Taking hoarfrost pictures on my phone during my morning break may give me joy, but to no one else if I don't share them. Joy was never meant to be hoarded (see what I did there?).

Jesus' love is the same way. It must be shared, and I can't fear offending, being misunderstood, or boring my readers (be aware, yes, because writing is also a skill that requires a lot of practice). Doing so only means I would rather keep my eyes closed and prevent others from seeing what I see.

I am no good to God that way. He gives us our gifts not for ourselves alone, but for others who need them even more than we do.

"You are the light of the world. A town built on a hill cannot be hidden. Neither do people light a lamp and put it under a bowl. Instead they put it on its stand, and it gives light to everyone in the house. In the same way, let your light shine before others, that they may see your good deeds and glorify your Father in heaven."
~ Matthew 5:14-16 (NIV)

NOT A COMPETITION

(April 15, 2018)

From the moment we're born, we compete with someone or something.

Children compete with siblings for parental attention. They compete with other students for that prized spot on the sports team.

Adults compete with others for employment, colleges, and for a potential spouse.

Competition is a great motivator. It encourages us to better ourselves.

The constant need to compete, however, also forces us to compare ourselves to others.

The hardest lesson I ever learned is how I will never be the best at anything. Someone will always be better—no matter how hard I work.

A trap I still fall into is how I translate failed comparisons to being a failure in my own eyes. And in God's eyes. Instead of pushing me to work harder and better myself, I allow feelings of failure to tempt me to quit. "I will never be the best, so how can I be any good to anyone?"

That may be what the world believes, but God's perspective is higher, longer, and deeper. I may never reach a million people with my words, but that's because God may prefer I reach fewer but a more select group. Reaching them doesn't make me a failure, but a success in God's eyes.

In the end, isn't God's perspective more important than our own and this world's? As long as we do the work God gives us to the best of our ability, we can never call ourselves a failure.

"Pay careful attention to your work, for then you will get the satisfaction of a job well done, and you won't need to compare yourself to anyone else. For we are each responsible for our own conduct."

~Galatians 6:4-5 (NLT)

APATHY

I'm suffering from a severe case of apathy.

Either I'm not getting enough sunlight, my hormones are completely whacked out, or it's a combination of both.

I'm not sad or depressed, but I can't seem to find a reason to care about much of anything more than what I'm required to do for work and family. I'm either in automatic or neutral, and I don't care enough to change gears even when I know I should.

I keep thinking I should be concerned, but I'm not. Mostly. Actually, I am concerned, but not enough to do anything about it.

Part of why I'm writing it down is so that maybe, just maybe doing so will push me out of this odd mood. Sometimes seeing what I'm thinking and feeling on the page helps me to find a solution to whatever is bugging me.

Change o' subject (sort of):

I'm thinking of changing the name of my blog again. Currently it's "Andra's Blog, A Writer's Journey." A more appropriate name might be "Dear God. I Have Questions."

Two reasons for this.

Once again I volunteered to write several devotions for my church's yearly Lenten devotional. Eight, actually, which is the most I've volunteered to write so far. In one of them I admitted I don't love or trust God as much as I know I should. I take much of my faith for granted, and worse, when it starts to matter, I hide it away, afraid.

Many non-religious accuse religious people, Christians especially, as following blindly, never asking challenging questions. For some, that's probably true. I've heard enough stories where church leaders have punished people in a variety of ways for daring to challenge their beliefs or orthodoxy.

Yet that's far from biblical. In both the Old and New Testaments, God and Jesus encouraged questions and seemed to enjoy being challenged (as long as the questioner was genuine in wanting to learn). For example, in the Old Testament Jacob literally wrestled with God (which is why God renamed him Israel or "one who struggles with God"). In the New Testament, never once did Jesus condemn anyone for asking questions. Sure, he was tough on the Pharisees (and on the apostles at times when they were being particularly thick-headed), but he also knew their motives. Their questions were meant to trap him, not to learn.

I want to focus my writing on studying God's word to strengthen my relationship with him. I also want to show others that part of being a Christian is to ask a lot of questions, to challenge our current religious thinking, and yes, to question what the Bible says about objectionable or problematic subjects (while at the same time knowing our understanding of said scripture is what's flawed, not the passages themselves).

I also hope that increasing my time of study will kick me out of this apathetic funk.

A LITTLE NUMBERS GAME

(February 18, 2020)

I wrote this back in 2006, so some of this will be a bit dated. I share it again, because I think it's important to remember.

$$10,005 - 1 \neq -10,006.$$

Or for the non-mathy people: 10,005 minus one does not equal negative 10,006.

That's an obvious statement, but I think we all tend to forget it.

I'm not talking about numbers, but negative critiques, rejections, or harsh comments.

My pastor last Sunday did a sermon on "The DaVinci Code."[1] I don't know exactly what happened since I wasn't there, but this is the gist of what I heard:

After he gave his sermon, someone approached and commented at how it wasn't appropriate to do a sermon on a fictional book.

Whether the person meant it harshly, I don't know. But my pastor's reaction is important. He took the comment so hard that in between the 8am and 9:30am services, he kneeled before the altar and wept.

I know he had to be thinking he made a terrible mistake by preaching on that subject. I'm sure he completely forgot any positive comments people gave him. Top that off with having to do the same sermon two more times. I doubt I could have pulled it off.

Why is it so easy to wrap our entire mind around one negative comment and ignore all the other 10,005 positive comments as if they never happened?

I wish I had an answer to that, because I do it all the time. It's a grueling mental wrestling match to convince me otherwise.

So I use this entry to encourage you to ignore the comments that hurt and embrace the ones that uplift (as well as consider the source; not everyone has your best interests at heart). I bet the positives outnumber the negatives in almost every case.

---

[1] "The DaVinci Code" by Dan Brown, Doubleday, ©2003

GIVE ME A REASON

(March 18, 2020)

I don't like to post scripture unless I can apply it to a real-world situation. I want to see the same thing when others post scripture: Why did they think that passage was so important to share? How is it relevant to their life and perhaps mine, too?

A few days ago, I wrote a long entry about how, as a whole, people are anxious to the point of extreme stress and holding onto those feelings (as well as acting on them) is doing more harm than good. Two days later and I apparently wasted my time. No one responded, and people are more anxious and more stressed than before. I fear no amount of scripture or real-world examples will make any difference—even amongst Christians.

I often point out the only thing in this world I can control is me. This is true for everyone. People will do what they will do, and this world will do what it will do. I am but one person out of eight billion, so how could I even dare to believe my words will make a difference? In other words, me posting on social media has as much positive effect as Grandpa Simpson[2] yelling at the clouds.

Yet I try, and yet I hope, because that's who I am—eternally optimistic.

And if you thought I would refrain from posting an applicable biblical passage or two at the end of this, boy were you wrong.

"But you, take courage! Do not let your hands be weak, for your work shall be rewarded."

~ 2 Chronicles 15:7 (ESV)

"And let us not grow weary of doing good, for in due season we will reap, if we do not give up."

~ Galatians 6:9

---

[2] From Season 13, Episode 13: "Old Man and the Key" of "The Simpsons"
Gracie Films, 20th Century Fox Television, 20th Television Animation ©2002

THE MIGHTY PEN

(June 1, 2020)

A few days ago, my hubby and I met with some friends at a restaurant. Most of the conversation circled around firearms, but then it turned toward other subjects such as the riots and other issues and controversies of the day.

Soon the conversation focused on social media.

One mentioned how he doesn't always agree with what I write on Facebook[3]. He considers responding but ends up leaving no comment. He said my posts are so well written, anything he adds would look stupid by comparison. "I simply don't know how to write with as good of grammar as you do."

Aside and disclaimer: this is not meant as a braggadocios post but something else, which I will explain further.

I quirked by head at him and said, "Huh. I never thought of using good grammar as a weapon before."

"That's exactly what it is," he said. "A weapon."

Another piped up with, "The pen is mightier than the sword after all."

The problem with some cliches is they often become so common, they take on a certain abstraction. I've used the pen versus sword phrase before, usually to say that we need to ever be aware of every word we speak or write. They can tear people down as easily as they can uplift.

Yet I still never considered writing well (having good grammar) as a weapon to the point people wouldn't want to engage—feeling inadequate to the task.

In some ways I was gratified by the comment, but it also made me sad. I never want to intimidate with my skills. I want to use them to invite and inform, so people will engage even if they disagree. Sometimes especially if they disagree. I would rather look like a fool for

---

[3] Social media platform: www.facebook.com

a moment than a fool forever because I didn't take the time to listen and learn something new.

I get it though.

I like to sing and love to belt out tunes while in my car or alone in the house. I may even be fairly good at it. I also don't know how to read a single note of music. I couldn't distinguish a B from an A to save my life.

If a professional singer asked me to do a duet, however, I would have to politely decline. I'm simply not skilled enough—feeling inadequate to the task. 'Tis better to sit in the corner and not engage.

At the same time, by not taking up the invitation, I would deny myself the benefit of the singer's skills and improve my own.

Sure, in some instances I like the idea of wielding my grammar skills as a weapon. Yet I prefer to wield them to teach and edify, but mostly as an invitation to discuss ideas and learn from others.

ILL WILL

(June 16, 2021)

I normally don't hold grudges. Doing so doesn't necessarily hurt the person I'm angry at, but it always hurts me. Holding on to anger is akin to living in the past, preventing me from enjoying the present and looking forward to the future.

Yet I'm doing exactly that. A few months back I discovered several co-workers acting in an unprofessional manner, made worse by the fact I still have to work with them and act professional when I want to do anything but.

I can't wait for the day I no longer have to interact or work with any of them. Ever. Again.

In short, while I may never outwardly show my contempt as much as may want to, I look forward to, at the very least, giving them my indifference.

As of now, though, my attitude is so sour, I find myself wishing—praying even—for them to fail at everything they do. I want others to see what I see and abandon them. I want their reputation to take such a spectacular dive, no one else will ever want to work with them, either.

I know what you're thinking: That's not very Christ-like of me. After all, does not God love them as much as he loves me? Does God hold his mercy and grace back simply because this piddly little human is angry? The idea is utter foolishness when seen from that perspective, isn't it?

While my heart is a rabid animal gnawing at the bars of its cage, growling to be let loose to rip apart and devour those who hurt me, my brain is holding the door closed, whispering calm. Reminding my heart that grace, mercy, and forgiveness are always the best roads to travel.

God never wishes me ill will no matter what I've done, so I can do no less.

Nor am I supposed to wait until I no longer have to deal with someone in order to do so. God wants us to forgive when it matters most, because he forgives us when it matters most.

"Let no corrupting talk come out of your mouths, but only such as is good for building up, as fits the occasion, that it may give grace to those who hear. And do not grieve the Holy Spirit of God, by whom you were sealed for the day of redemption. Let all bitterness and wrath and anger and clamor and slander be put away from you, along with all malice. Be kind to one another, tenderhearted, forgiving one another, as God in Christ forgave you."

~ Ephesians 4:29-32 (ESV)

LUDDITE?[4] OR JUST OLD?

(September 18, 2022)[5]

Not all of my entries are profound or have any take-away value. Sometimes a little levity is needed. This be one of them. Enjoy!

A few weeks ago, a friend's teenage son backed into my car and dented the rear side panel. Her insurance paid for everything, including a rental car for the three days my car was in the shop for repairs.

I own a 2013 Toyota FJ Cruiser. Manual transmission. Keep that in mind.

The rental was a 2020 Ford Edge. Automatic transmission. We looked it over for a few minutes to make note of any existing dings or scratches so we wouldn't be blamed for them when we returned it. The customer service rep also started it to make sure everything functioned, and it had a full tank of gas. Once done, she turned off the car, handed me the dongle (button start, no key needed), and walked away.

I sat in the driver's seat and pressed the start button. All the electronics turned on and the seat moved forward.

But the engine didn't start.

Huh. I pressed the start button again and the seat moved back. Still no engine start.

So I tried again. The seat moved forward again, but still the engine remained silent. I tried this several times before asking my husband what I was doing wrong.

He couldn't figure it out for a few seconds until he asked, "Is your foot on the brake?"

Oh, yeah. That's a thing with automatic transmissions. Having driven a manual transmission for the last nine years, I had forgotten that little bit of know-how.

Sure enough, once I engaged the brake, the car started right up.

---

[4] Luddite: one of a group of early 19th century English workmen destroying laborsaving machinery as a protest, or more broadly: one who is opposed to especially technological change

[5] On a whim I submitted this to the Writers Digest 92nd Annual Writing Competition for the humor category. It earned an honorable mention.

I wish I could say my confusion ended there.

Instead of a standard lever gear-shifter, it had a knob. I studied it for a bit to figure out how many times to I needed to turn it to get from "Park" to "Drive."

Once I figured it out, I left the rental parking lot, completely confident I had figured everything out.

Going back to work went well.

Mostly.

Until I realized the steering wheel was a little too high for me. On my car, the adjuster is a little lever on the steering column. I searched for something similar on the Edge.

No lever.

I did, however, see this little button with a "+" sign. So I pushed it.

Not a steering wheel adjuster. It was a gear shifter, and by pressing it, the car went from gear four to gear three. I pressed it again thinking it would raise the gear. Nope. I went down to first gear, and the poor engine is now screaming at me.

So I went the next several blocks with the engine sounding like a single-cylinder dirt bike until it switched gears on its own.

Only after I arrived at work did I finally see the other little button with a "-" sign on the other side of the steering wheel.

I wish I could say my confusion ended there.

The next morning, I went to a local coffee shop before work. As I left the parking lot, I noticed the rear windshield wiper was on. No idea how I turned it on, let alone know how to turn the darn thing off. I'm sure the people behind me thought I was an idiot (and they wouldn't have been wrong) as I flipped switches and turned knobs making the wipers go faster, slower, sprayed windshield wiper fluid (more than once), faster again, slower again. I finally gave up and drove the rest of the way to work with that wiper swishing back and forth during a perfectly warm and sunny day.

When I arrived at work, I went to YouTube and searched for a video on how to use windshield wipers on a 2020 Ford Edge. Turns out it was a tiny switch on the tip of the windshield wiper lever.

Thankfully, my confusion did end there, but I also didn't chance making a further fool out of myself on the road by testing any of the other electronics. Not even the radio.

I've always thought of myself as rather tech-savvy, but a two-year old car showed this fifty-plus-year-old woman a far different reality.

A SLAP UPSIDE THE HEAD

(January 1, 2023)

We all face slings and arrows in life, and they often hit us where it hurts the most.

Last year someone filed a complaint against my land surveyor's license. After months of back-and-forth, I was given a reprimand for several ethics violations. Namely not being clear enough with my words when speaking before a public board. It could have been worse, but at the same time, the arrow hit just the right spot. In this case, my confidence.

How can a wordsmith claim to be any good if he/she faces literal prosecution for not being clear enough with those words?

But God is patient. He allows us time to grieve, to consider (See Ecclesiastes 3:1-8). Perhaps even a bit of self-pity, although I've discovered he has less patience for that.

Oddly enough I'm grateful for the entire experience. For one, I will now be even more careful with my words in the future—whether written or otherwise.

I was also required to take eight hours of online ethics courses as a part of the reprimand. I finished the required eight hours, plus two extra within two weeks when I had twelve months to comply.

I didn't stop there, though. In my search for ethics courses, I found a business ethics certification course through Cornell University[6]. I decided to sign up for that one as well, but I did it for myself, to learn something new. I just completed the second course of four, and that's partly why I've not been writing any entries. Although not really, because the course requirements don't take up *that* much of my time.

So why do I write an entry now, and why did I choose this specific title?

Because, according to God, my time of self-pity and grief is done.

---

[6] https://ecornell.cornell.edu/certificates/law/business-ethics/

I've been watching "The Chosen"[7] through the Angel[8] app. Along with "The Chosen" are other series, so I decided to watch one called "The Testament." It's about the Book of Acts, but it takes place in more modern times. The main character is Luke (who wrote the Gospel of Luke as well as Acts).

In the last scene Peter finds a net in the grass and tells Luke about how Jesus called him, a fisherman, to be a fisher of men. He then said (paraphrased) "Your writing is your net to share the story of Jesus."

How can this writer, who hasn't been writing much, not be convicted by that? Or to put it another way, he used that scene to figuratively slap me upside the head.

I don't intend to compare myself to the writers of the New Testament, let alone the gospels. Perish the thought!

But when God gives us a talent, our duty is to not let it flounder. Certainly not because of a moment of self-pity.

---

[7] Thechosen.tv
[8] Angel.com

PART 2: CULTURE

KILL LANGUAGE, KILL FREEDOM

(February 21, 2017)

I love watching my son grow up. What parent doesn't, right? The best part for me is how he develops, especially when it comes to language. When he was still a toddler, I was astounded at how quickly he picked up concepts and how they all tied to language. For instance, I showed him an apple, and said, "This is an apple." He understood right away what I meant. He also didn't get confused when I taught him colors. I pointed to a red apple to show him "red," and he easily grasped the difference between "red" and "apple." I realized then that language is built into our brains and develops naturally as we grow up.

Language keeps us connected and helps us learn about the world. Without language, we couldn't build anything (consider the Tower of Babel in Genesis 11:1-9). Imagine trying to build a house with others without the ability to communicate.

Aside: Even math and music are considered languages, and while some believe they can do without math, most everyone needs music.

Mess with language and we mess with the free exchange of ideas. People no longer understand their world or each other, and we can no longer grow as a species.

George Orwell understood this better than most. He conveyed his concerns in an essay titled "Politics and the English Language."[9]

He dug deeper and expressed it more in his book, "1984,"[10] most specifically with the language he labeled as "Newspeak."

According to a website dedicated to Orwell[11]: "The whole aim of Newspeak is to narrow the range of thought."

---

[9] https://www.orwell.ru/library/essays/politics/english/e_polit

[10] "1984" by George Orwell, originally published in 1949 (Historical side note: He wrote it in 1948 and merely switched the 4 and the 8 to come up with the title).

[11] www.orwelltoday.com/newspeak.shtml

To expand the idea (on the same webpage): "Newspeak was the official language of Oceania and had been devised to meet the ideological needs of Ingsoc, or English Socialism. In the year 1984 there was not as yet anyone who used Newspeak as his sole means of communication, either in speech or writing. The leading articles in The Times were written in it, but could only be carried out by a specialist. It was expected that Newspeak would have finally superseded Oldspeak (or Standard English) by about the year 2050. Meanwhile it gained ground steadily, all Party members tending to use Newspeak words and grammatical constructions more and more in their everyday speech."

I ran into an article earlier today at the Daily Caller[12] which in turn led me to the University of Washington/Tacoma's University Writing Program and their Writing Center[13].

Under "Our Beliefs" of their "Statement on Antiracist and Social Justice Work in the Writing Center" it states: "The writing center works from several important beliefs that are crucial to helping writers write and succeed in a racist society. The racist conditions of our society are not simply a matter of bias or prejudice that some people hold. In fact, most racism, for instance, is not accomplished through intent. Racism is the normal condition of things. Racism is pervasive. It is in the systems, structures, rules, languages, expectations, and guidelines that make up our classes, school, and society. For example, linguistic and writing research has shown clearly for many decades that there is no inherent 'standard' of English. Language is constantly changing. These two facts make it very difficult to justify placing people in hierarchies or restricting opportunities and privileges because of the way people communicate in particular versions of English."

I'm sure you can see the correlation between Newspeak and what the writing center is espousing.

---

[12] http://dailycaller.com/2017/02/20/college-writing-center-declares-american-grammar-a-racist-unjust-language-structure/
[13] https://www.tacoma.uw.edu/tlc/writing-center. NOTE: to see the statement one must sign up.

What led me on this journey (thanks to author LK Hunsaker[14]) is an article by the Chicago Tribune[15].

According to the article, some publishers are hiring so-called sensitivity readers "who, for a nominal fee, will scan the book for racist, sexist or otherwise offensive content. These readers give feedback based on self-ascribed areas of expertise such as 'dealing with terminal illness,' 'racial dynamics in Muslim communities within families' or 'transgender issues.'"

These statements are of special concern: "Sensitivity readers have emerged in a climate—fueled in part by social media—in which writers are under increased scrutiny for their portrayals of people from marginalized groups, especially when the author is not a part of that group."

And: "It feels like I'm supplying the seeds and the gems and the jewels from our culture, and it creates cultural thievery," Clayton [a sensitivity reader] said. "Why am I going to give you all of those little things that make my culture so interesting so you can go and use it and you don't understand it?"

Also known as "cultural appropriation."

Aside: for me personally, I don't care who writes about my culture, as long as they do so accurately. Not every person wants to write about their culture, so why limit themselves, and in the end possibly dooming their culture's future to oblivion because no one dared, or was allowed to, write about it?

Another aside: the article included this: "Despite the efforts of groups like We Need Diverse Books, 'it's more likely that a publishing house will publish a book about an African-American girl by a white woman versus one written by a black woman like me,' Clayton says."

During my own search of literary agents, I had to cross out quite a few because they are actively seeking so-called marginalized writers

---

[14] lkhunsaker.com

[15] https://www.chicagotribune.com/entertainment/books/ct-publishers-hiring-book-readers-to-flag-sensitivity-20170215-story.html

such as Ms. Clayton. I am not a member, so I believe she's incorrect in her assessment.

Agents still, in the end, care most about the story and the quality of writing (EDIT: At least I hope this is still true. For the most part, though, more readers than not care about the story and not the author's skin color, beliefs, and/or political persuasion).

Even those agents and publishers seeking minorities still need a salable story, so although a person's minority status may get them to the front of the line, he/she still has to deliver. Seems to me, Ms. Clayton is holding herself back and using her race and gender as an excuse not to try, let alone succeed. Too harsh? Offensive even? Good.

Now back to the original subject.

All of this is political correctness [now dubbed "wokeism"] not only run amok but an attempt to control thought. When you control how language is used—eliminating certain words or changing the definition of words in order to change peoples' perception—you can control how a person thinks. When you control how someone thinks, that person loses their freedom to consider otherwise. They can no longer reason, because, in a sense, their words are chosen for them. The number of words—and ideas—they can use are curtailed if not outright eliminated.

If I offend you, or if you offend me, all the better. To quote (where it originated, I don't know): "The solution to offensive speech is more speech, not less."

Writers especially need to protect all words and language—our tools of trade. We can't allow any type of censorship, because once it grabs hold, we may lose everything.

Truth is most often found in offensive speech, because it forces us to think and respond. We human beings are experts at lying to ourselves and lying to each other. By attempting to control words and speech, the truth gets lost and liars rule at the expense of everyone else.

THE SCIENCE OF MORALITY

(August 11, 2017)

When thinking of the natural world—science if you will—we rarely tie morality into it. They should be mutually exclusive, because science is the study of the natural world, whereas morality is a construct invented by man (or God depending on your beliefs) in order to create a civil society.

I watched a video[16] where a philosopher contorted herself into a mental pretzel while describing how some "early fetuses" have no moral status[17] when others do. As such, according to her, abortion is not a moral issue.

Aside: This post isn't about abortion, per se, but about how biological knowledge can and should, in many circumstances, define our morality.

At no time did the philosopher mention biology. Nor did the two men interviewing her ask how a "wanted" fetus differs biologically from an "unwanted" fetus. Then again, if they had, her argument would have collapsed.

And they couldn't have that now, could they?

This in turn reminded me of another conversation with someone who argued that biology and laws have no bearing on each other, especially when it comes to human rights.

I responded, "Biology has everything to do with it. For instance, we don't give monkeys or dogs the same rights as humans. Why? Because they're not biologically human."

Humans have known this almost instinctively for thousands of years, even though they had no idea what a cell looked like. Nor did they have any concept of a DNA strand that more definitively proves the differences between all species whether animal, plant, or other.

---

[16] https://youtu.be/r5SQnQjryzI

[17] Someone once asked what the philosopher meant by "moral status." Think of a car. It's a thing that only has as much worth as the owner places on it. If an owner takes it to a junkyard, who cares? Therefore its mere existence can't have any *inherent* moral value.

I'll even wager most of our morals *depend* on our understanding of the natural world. They should be, and will always remain, intrinsically linked.

A few months ago, I read portions of Leviticus. Many find it dry and boring, because it contains laws about holiness, ritual cleanliness, family life, and a slew of others.

I discovered many of the laws, especially with regard to sanitation, we apply and take for granted today. The difference is, we do those things not for religious reasons, but because we now understand the science of how diseases spread.

If we choose to ignore biology and try to make a "moral" stance based on how we *think* our biology should be instead of what it is, we do so at our own peril.

That society is trying to erase what it means to be human, man, woman, boy, and girl became abundantly clear with the reaction to the release of the so-called "Google memo."[18] I encourage you to read it and not depend on my opinion of it (or anyone else's for that matter, including the writer of the memo).

Mr. James Damore (who wrote the memo) made a valid point, which many scientists have proven time and again: Men and women are different. Men—on average—react one way to a particular situation, and women—on average—react another way. One isn't necessarily better or worse than the other. It should show, however, that men and women complement each other. Where one is weak, the other is strong, and vice-versa. When we work together as partners with different roles to play, we can accomplish great things.

In short, trying to make women and men and boys and girls the same (or try to change into a different sex), we both ignore and destroy what makes each beautiful, unique, and strong. Morally, we should acknowledge, encourage, and embrace our biological differences, because if we don't, we will, in the end, destroy each other and ourselves.

---

[18] http://gizmodo.com/exclusive-heres-the-full-10-page-anti-diversity-screed-1797564320

WORDS OF WAR

(August 18, 2017)

As a writer I'm supposed to love words. Every single one of them, even if they're offensive. In fact, offensive words require more protection than those that don't. If we erase offensive words[19], we erase what makes us human, both the icky and the beautiful. After all, if we don't acknowledge what makes us evil, we can never change and bring about good.

Yet I am as human as the next person. While I can't think of a word I hate, there are many phrases I do hate. Some of them are due to overuse. Clichés if you will. I am guilty of using them as much as the next person, but I find we use them more out of habit which requires little to no critical thought. Call it a verbal knee-jerk reaction.

One particular cliché raises my hackles every time: I'm entitled to my opinion.

I have and never will tell anyone they are not entitled to their opinion, certainly not to try to take away their ability to express it. Admittedly, some of my statements can be inferred that way, but is that my fault, or the reader's? Maybe both, but this entry is to explain why, just because someone infers that I don't want them to speak out, in my case it's never implied. I will always welcome opposing views, because whatever the subject matter, it's an opportunity to learn something new, and I could very well be wrong in my suppositions.

It's better to be wrong for a moment than be wrong for a lifetime.

I also think people use the statement as a way of shutting the door on a conversation or debate. It's understandable, granted. Sometimes we don't want to engage in debate. We simply want to express our view and walk away.

However, when we do it on a public forum, we must expect others will respond. That's why it's called social media.

---

[19] Except so-called offensive words are in constant flux. What was inoffensive yesterday can be considered offensive today.

Freedom of expression is a swinging doorway. It means that while people have the right to express themselves, other people with differing views also have the right to respond.

When someone says, "I'm entitled to my opinion," for me, it's attempting to shut that door and lock it, or make it swing only one way, so people on the other side can't get in. Now if they want to say, "We'll have to agree to disagree," or "I understand your opinion, but I don't share it," or other variations thereof, that's different. While both effectively end debate, it's not telling the other person to shut up as if their opinion has lesser value.

My love of words is what makes me so sensitive with how they're structured and used. Words can be weapons that hurt and destroy as easily as they heal, inspire, and encourage. Like a loaded firearm, we need to be eternally aware and vigilant on how we wield them.

IS THERE AN ECHO IN HERE?

(September 24, 2017)

The easiest temptation on social media is to follow people, blogs, websites, etc. who reinforce what we already believe.

More difficult is to follow those who have near the opposite point of view. When we do, however, it's usually to laugh, scoff, or take offense. We don't do it to learn and listen but to argue—sometimes in the hopes of convincing the opposition of the rightness of our cause.

Yet the opposition often has no more desire to listen and learn than we do. In the end we give up and return to our own little echo chambers.

I don't often read articles on sites such as Vox, Slate, or Salon. I find their sites rife with too much bias for my taste.

Sometimes, however, I run into a headline that so intrigues me (and not in a good way), that I have to read it.

This is one such headline: "It's Time to Give Up on Facts." Subtitle: "Or at least to temporarily lay them down in favor of a more useful weapon: emotions."[20]

When I debate or discuss, I make sure I have truth and facts to back me up, otherwise, not only will I fail to convince, but I waste my time and that of my opposition. I don't argue with emotions, because emotions are not rational or logical. Too often they are baseless and fleeting and based on a misunderstanding of a smattering of facts. As such they can do more harm than good when trying to debate.

As conservative commentator Ben Shapiro likes to say, "Facts don't care about your feelings."

You can now understand why I found this headline so befuddling. Why would anyone give up facts in favor of emotion to win people to their side? It's idiocy.

Out of morbid curiosity, I decided to read the piece. Too many news websites love to write provocative headlines in order to get

---

[20] https://slate.com/technology/2017/02/counter-lies-with-emotions-not-facts.html

people to read it (such as me). Click-bait as it's called. Often, however, the headlines can be misleading, and the article is, in fact, making the opposite point.

Not this article, though. I objected to much of it such as using emotions as a weapon. It implies that the author doesn't want to convince, but to manipulate. It read less like a professional article and more like a personal journal entry (kind of like this lovely entry). The author wasn't trying to make a specific point but exploring his/her thoughts in order to discover that point.

Still, after weeding through all the verbosity, I surmised the author's overall point was not to give up on facts, per se, but to appeal to a person's emotions with facts instead of presenting facts alone. It's a valid point. In this day and age, regardless of what side people take on an issue, they are so emotionally entrenched in their point of view, facts proving their contentions false won't deter them.

It's worth thinking about, and for me, will be one heck of a challenge. Only facts matter to me, because they're immutable. Still, to see the other person's emotional point of view and try to understand it before I can debate a specific issue is important.

I have to learn how to speak their emotional language, otherwise communication will be near impossible.

If I hadn't stepped out of my own self-imposed echo chamber, I wouldn't have discovered, let alone considered the idea.

NOT MY TRIBE

(September 28, 2019)

We live in an era in the States where people have tribalized themselves. At first glance it's not a terrible thing. That we seek to spend our time with those who share the same interests and points-of-view is a natural part of being human. We want to be loved, respected, and understood. Generally speaking, we're terrified of feeling isolated, especially in a group of strangers who think, behave, and believe differently.

Unfortunately, we've taken that natural tendency to the point of seeing those of un-like mind as an enemy. We see those differences as a threat to our own worldview, perhaps even our very way of life. As such, we no longer want to simply separate ourselves, but to destroy those who aren't a member of our chosen tribe.

One of my pet-peeves is when people misuse scripture. Two misused verses in particular make me grind my teeth:

> *"... if God is for us, who can be against us?"*
>
> ~ Romans 8:31b (ESV)

> *"Whoever is not with me is against me, and whoever does not gather with me scatters."*
>
> ~ Matthew 12:30

As to the first verse, there's one word that people tend to gloss over: If. Some believe that since they're doing God's work, anyone who disagrees or actively fights against them are going against God. They must therefore be God's enemy. However, they too often forget to ask (or ignore) if they're actually doing God's will before making that claim.

They often use the second verse to bolster their point of view, but they again forget (or ignore) that Jesus is talking about himself. No follower of Jesus, or any other human, can claim it for themselves.

Jesus said, "You have heard that it was said, 'You shall love your neighbor and hate your enemy.' But I say to you, Love your enemies and pray for those who persecute you."

~ Matthew 5:43-44

A scribe once asked Jesus what the greatest commandment was. He responded:

"The most important is, 'Hear, O Israel: The Lord our God, the Lord is one. And you shall love the Lord your God with all your heart and with all your soul and with all your mind and with all your strength.' The second is this: 'You shall love your neighbor as yourself.' There is no other commandment greater than these."

~ Mark 12:29-31

When I see all this tribalism and hatred or contempt of anyone not within that tribe, I not only think of the scripture above, but ask myself how God sees it all. Can we really expect God to take our side over another's? Would a parent take the side of one child over another's when they fight? Perhaps to the point of calling the other child an enemy deserving of death?

God hates none of his children, and because he calls us to be like him, we must love our enemies—real or imagined—no matter what tribe they belong to (see Isaiah 56:3-8 and Galatians 3:28).

GROWTH ON A CONCRETE PAST

(January 28, 2020)

Jesus said we must love our enemies. Many verses (both Old and New Testament) describe what that looks like.

From the Old Testament:

"When you encounter your enemy's ox or ass wandering, you must take it back to him. When you see the ass of your enemy lying under its burden and would refrain from raising it, you must nevertheless raise it with him."

~ Exodus 23:4-5 (JPS)

"If your enemy is hungry, give him bread to eat;
If he is thirsty, give him water to drink.
You will be heaping live coals on his head,
And the Lord will reward you."

~ Proverbs 25:21-22

From the New Testament:

"But I say to you who hear, Love your enemies, do good to those who hate you, bless those who curse you, pray for those who abuse you."

~ Luke 6:27-28 (ESV)

"So whatever you wish that others would do to you, do also to them, for this is the Law and the Prophets."

~ Matthew 7:12

Social media is an unforgiving place. It's been around long enough that things we've written a decade ago are still around for people to see—and judge. People far too often find themselves being condemned. Some have lost their jobs, college scholarships, homes, and family. Others were so destroyed, they ended up killing themselves.

Not one of their "judges" took into consideration the person might have grown and changed.

Too many don't know or refuse to apply the Golden Rule (Matthew 7:12), especially when it comes to entertainers, politicians, and other famous people. Based on past bad acts (real or merely accused), when they do something good, we automatically assume their motives are impure. We condemn them regardless—as if we can know their mind and it'll be forever unchanged.

I'll bet if you were to go through everything I've written, you'll find many mistakes, yet I have since changed my mind. I would hope that anyone who reads my words would at least give me the benefit of the doubt and ask if I still feel that way.

When people we love and respect do something wrong, our first thought is, "Why would they do such a thing?" We don't automatically ascribe bad motive and condemn them.

We need to do better in giving people—all people—room to grow. We can't change the past, but we can change our mind and learn from our mistakes. So, too, can our enemies. Because, like it or not, everyone has enemies. I also think we hope even our enemies would love us as Jesus loves us—and give us equal benefit of the doubt when our wrongdoing is brought to light. Just like our loved ones do.

No one is above—or below—that level of grace. Jesus did that for us, and he expects us to do the same.

WHO ARE YOU?

(March 25, 2020)

In good times, putting on a mask for others is easy. We want to look like we're all together, happy, and content. Part of it is not wanting to burden others—to be a "wet blanket" so to speak. The biggest reason, however, is pride. We want to show the world we're better than we are. No one likes to admit their shortfalls, mistakes, and weaknesses.

That "perfect" mask we also keep on for our own benefit. We humans are experts at deceiving ourselves.

When troubled times hit, however, that mask falls away, and we can no longer hide from the real face in the mirror.

I saw a meme a few days ago that said, "I guess God got so mad about all of our fighting down here that he sent us all to our rooms."

Funny, but true in a way. When parents send children to their room for misbehaving, they do so in the hope the children will contemplate what they did wrong and figure out how to do better next time.

I, for one, saw a glimpse of who I am with regard to facing troubles not of my making, and ones for which I have no immediate solution. Like so many others, I am at the mercy of my own government telling me what I can and cannot do, where I can and cannot go, and with whom I am allowed and not allowed to spend my time.[21]

The rebel in me had a two-week long temper tantrum (as anyone who's been reading my blog as well as my Twitter and/or Facebook feeds can attest).

With my mask now shattered at my feet, I must face the awful truth: I've yet to take my own advice.

---

[21] For historical context, this was when local, state, and federal governments shut down everything including most private businesses and churches under the guise of "slowing the spread" of the virus known as COVID-19. Other restrictions and/or mandates included wearing masks, limiting all get-togethers to a few people, and so-called social distancing where people had to stay a minimum of six feet from everyone else.

When stripped of all pretense and deception, who I am is a spoiled, angry hypocrite.

Nor am I unique. I keep thinking of the Israelites when, in the book of Exodus, God rescued them out of Egypt. Talk about complainers! No matter how well God took care of their needs, it was never enough.

One of my favorite passages was when the Israelites reached the Red Sea and saw the Egyptians marching after them. They screamed at Moses that they were better off as slaves in Egypt, because at least there they wouldn't be massacred.

I don't think they feared the Egyptians so much as the unknown. As slaves, they knew what their future held. Heading toward an unknown wilderness—even freely—can be a terrifying idea.

We are in a similar—if figurative—unknown wilderness now. We can't help but ask, "When will this end? Will I have a job when it's all said and done, and even if I do, how do I feed my family and pay all my bills in the meantime?"

Many have said we need not fear, to trust God, and pray unceasingly. Moses said as much in Exodus 14:13-14 (ESV):

"Fear not, stand firm, and see the salvation of the LORD, which he will work for you today. For the Egyptians whom you see today, you shall never see again. The LORD will fight for you, and you have only to be silent."

I love God's response (verse 15):

"Why do you cry to me? Tell the people of Israel to go forward."

He then parted the Red Sea and delivered the Israelites from the Egyptians.

We should absolutely continue to pray and trust God without qualification, yet at the same time we need to listen. He might also be asking us to "go forward."

Regardless of what our government is doing (whether rightly or wrongly is a different discussion), we are not completely helpless or without means or resources. We may have to drop our masks in front of others and ask for help, while at the same time look for ways to help those with even fewer resources.

WHAT WOULD JESUS DO?

(May 25, 2020)

That was a popular question a few decades ago, further popularized by the acronym WWJD. It was a simple way to get people to think before they act, and with the hope they'd make the right decision. The phrase fell away rather quickly for many reasons. One of which is, can we really know what Jesus would do in any given circumstance?

That said, if I created a poll asking if Jesus were alive on earth today, would he wear a mask? I'll bet the results would be an even 50/50.

The fact our opinions would be split means we're asking the wrong question, and our motives for asking are improper. It's placing Jesus in the middle of an argument and demanding he take sides so we can point to the opposition and say, "See? You're wrong!"

Sure, no one I know of has asked this particular question, but they've asked others such as would Jesus be a Republican or a Democrat; would he approve of turning people away at the border; etc.

Regardless, Jesus won't take sides, because this is a human question, not a godly one.

Some at this point might say, "Aren't you assuming to know the mind of God here? How do you know he won't take sides? This is an important question!"

Sure, for us. Not for Jesus. Whether or not people wear a mask does not determine the health of their soul. Jesus won't assume someone wearing a mask knows and follows him anymore than someone not wearing a mask doesn't know or follow him. Eternally speaking, the question is irrelevant. He will ask instead, "Is your mind, body, and soul right with me?"

So what's the point of this entry? Is it about masks, what Jesus would do or not do, or something else?

We've been in a frenzy about a virus to the point of obsession for what feels like forever. No matter where we go or what we do, it's literally in our face. We can't escape it from the news, from social media, and at every gathering (online or in person) it's too often the main subject of discussion.

We need to stop and turn (or keep) our focus on Jesus. No matter what, whether it's a hurricane, earthquake, virus, or disease destroying our body, he's still in control and has our soul well in hand.

"Set your minds on the things that are above, not on things that are on earth. For you have died, and your life is hidden with Christ in God."
~ Colossians 3:2-3 (ESV)

"Not that I have already obtained this or am already perfect, but I press on to make it my own, because Christ Jesus has made me his own. Brothers, I do not consider that I have made it my own. But one thing I do: forgetting what lies behind and straining forward to what lies ahead, I press on toward the goal for the prize of the upward call of God in Christ Jesus."
~ Philippians 3:12-14

THE LIBERTY TO WALK AWAY

(November 7, 2020)

In previous entries, I've stated we sometimes need to look for what the Bible doesn't say. This is another such time.

One statement I'm hearing a lot lately is, "If you love your neighbor, you would do X."

Ever since I heard it the first time, it's been eating at me. Why am I so bothered about it? Is it not scriptural? After thinking about it for a few weeks, I finally understood.

The entire statement is absurd. Nor is it scriptural.

How's that for an audacious statement? Read on, and I'll explain why.

The scripture incorrectly referred to above actually says: "Love your neighbor as yourself." [22] What I call the biggest little word is missing: If. Meaning no qualifiers are attached.

Loving one's neighbor can take many forms, and yes it can include doing X if someone asks us to (the key word being "ask"). Yet some things we must never do.

One is to use force or the threat of force to make people do something or to act a certain way—such as through local or federal authorities.

The worst part of the statement is it implies that anyone who doesn't do X doesn't love their neighbor. As such, it's an attempt to shame people into compliance. That's coercion, something else one must never do.

Liberty is defined as:

- the state of being free within society from oppressive restrictions imposed by authority on one's way of life, behavior, or political views
- the state of not being imprisoned or enslaved

---

[22] This particular verse is mentioned many times in scripture including Leviticus 19:18, Matthew 22:39, and Galatians 5:14

- a right or privilege, especially a statutory one [such as the US Bill of Rights]
- the power or scope to act as one pleases

But what does the Bible say about liberty as well as loving one's neighbor? Are they mutually exclusive, or do they go hand-in-hand?

The story of the Good Samaritan is the oft-cited example of loving one's neighbor (Luke 10:25-37).

The Cliff-Notes version is a man is robbed, beaten, and left for dead. Three people encounter him: a priest, a Levite, and a Samaritan (it almost sounds like the beginning of a joke, doesn't it?). Only the Samaritan stops to help him.

So now we need to look for what's *not* said. In this case, no angel (nor God) came down and demanded any one of the men to stop and help. The story also doesn't include an authority forcing the three to act. Nor do the men turn to the authorities to force the other two to act.

They all had the option to walk away. Including the Samaritan.

Mark 10:17-22 (ESV) has been sticking with me lately:

As Jesus started on his way, a man ran up to him and fell on his knees before him. "Good teacher," he asked, "what must I do to inherit eternal life?"

"Why do you call me good?" Jesus answered. "No one is good—except God alone. You know the commandments: 'You shall not murder, you shall not commit adultery, you shall not steal, you shall not give false testimony, you shall not defraud, honor your father and mother.'"

"Teacher," he declared, "all these I have kept since I was a boy."

Jesus looked at him and loved him. "One thing you lack," he said. "Go, sell everything you have and give to the poor, and you will have treasure in heaven. Then come, follow me."

At this the man's face fell. He went away sad, because he had great wealth.

The key statement is in the last verse: "He went away sad…" Yet the verse "Jesus looked at him and loved him" is equally poignant.

Jesus loved him, and because of that, allowed him the choice—the liberty—to walk away even as it may have broken his heart to do so. He told the man the truth, and with conviction, which is important. But again, looking for what isn't said, he didn't threaten or force the man into changing his mind with local/worldly authorities or coerce through shame.

We are called to be just like Jesus, and that includes giving people the liberty to make their own choices, to walk away without us piling on threats or shame as they do so.

So in answer to the question above, loving one's neighbor *must* include liberty, no "ifs" about it.

We can't do one without giving the other.

"and to aspire to live quietly, and to mind your own affairs, and to work with your hands, as we instructed you, so that you may walk properly before outsiders and be dependent on no one."
~ 1 Thessalonians 4:11-12 (ESV)

THE NEW HEROISM

(March 15, 2021)

Warning: unpopular opinion ahead.

A few days ago I engaged in a Facebook discussion (I know, a contradiction in terms). A person said we shouldn't boycott businesses for the thing-that-shall-not-be-named[23], because it could potentially hurt her job. I jumped in as I'm often wont to do. As expected, she was a bit offended and basically said my life was likely unaffected by said thing-that-shall-not-be-named—unlike hers.

I started to respond with my own hardships but soon stopped and deleted it.

This wasn't a contest about who's the bigger victim.

For me it's always about truth, facts, and consequences, and as Ben Shapiro likes to say, "Facts don't care about your feelings." Nor do truth or consequences. At the beginning of my last comment, I instead wrote, "Read my comments with the head, not the heart."

That little exchange is an example of where we are today as a society. Not that we approach everything based on our feelings (although that's part of it), but we've chosen to treat some victims as heroes.

Oprah's recent interview with Britain's Prince Harry and Meghan Markle[24] is another example. I only saw excerpts, but what I did see was nothing but a "woe-is-me" session, and an expectation that Meghan deserves our adoration and respect because royal life is harder than she expected.

Let me add something before I go any further. This is not to minimize or mock anyone's pain or true victimization. Victims do need their voices heard, especially in a court of law. Only there can the perpetrator be stripped of his/her ability to victimize others.

---

[23] I used this phrase instead of "COVID" or "COVID-19" due to social media platforms constantly inundating my posts with so-called "fact checkers."

[24] https://www.youtube.com/watch?v=4Kj8UPnZfPc

This isn't about victims, either, but how society demands that in order to be heard, a person *must* be a victim.

The Facebook conversation above highlights that tendency. My opponent tried to silence me by basically saying, "You're not a victim of the thing-that-shall-not-be-named, so you have no right to speak about it."

One need not be a victim of an injustice or crime to opine on it. We all have a conscience, and most have an innate knowledge of right and wrong, good and evil. We not only have the *right* to say something, but the *duty.*

Being a victim does not make one an expert on a particular subject. It'd be like me saying that since I lost a tire hitting a pothole while crossing a bridge, I'm now an expert on road and bridge engineering.

I applaud everyone who's risen above their hardships with grace and determination—and humility. What I won't do is bow before them (figuratively or literally) or be expected to shut up because I've not faced the same hardship.

And neither should you or anyone else.

FOR THE LOVE OF…

(May 31, 2021)

I can't say I truly love language. If I did, I would have spent my life studying more than my native tongue and digging deeper into its intricacies. If anything, when I write, I do so largely by instinct. I can define few of its rules such as "dangling participle" without looking it up first.

I can say, however, I love the *idea* of it. I love how language can be used as a weapon as easily as it can heal. It brings people together and encourages creativity. It also causes wars and strife.

God loves language. He created the universe by speaking it into existence (Genesis 1:1-31 & Ps. 33:6). One of Jesus' names is the Word of God (John 1). Scripture warns us of its power to destroy as well as create (see Proverbs 11:9, 15:4, 16:24 & 18:21).

Yesterday while perusing Netflix[25], I saw the description of the movie (based on the book by the same name[26]), "The Professor and the Madman"[27]: Netflix described it thusly: "Completing the first dictionary will take a bit of smarts and a bit of madness. The words will come eventually."

I was, of course, intrigued.

The book and movie are about how the Oxford Dictionary was first written, the challenges of such a massive endeavor, and how it nearly failed without the help of a criminally insane murderer who alone submitted over ten thousand words.

Mel Gibson plays the professor, and Sean Penn plays the madman. Incredibly acted by both, and the dialog alone is fantastic. One quote in particular stuck with me: "… for every word in action becomes beautiful in the light of its own meaning."

---

[25] Television and movie internet streaming company: www.netflix.com

[26] "The Professor and the Madman" by Simon Winchester, Harper Collins Publishers; 6th Printing edition ©1998

[27] "The Professor and the Madman" Voltage Pictures, Fábrica de Cine, Definition Films, ©2019

Words matter; their definitions equally so. Without their definitions and etymology (origin), they become flat if not ultimately meaningless—a bunch of letters strung together and nothing else.

Which is why I get particularly grumpy when people, our government, and other powers that be—including the current Oxford Dictionary publisher, ironically enough—try to erase or ban words, or change their meaning to either make them meaningless or the direct opposite of their origin.

We must protect words and their definition/origins as we would anything else we hold dear.

HOW OLD IS THE UNIVERSE?

(November 7, 2021)

There are two major camps with regard to the age of the universe. Some believe, based on the genealogies listed in the Old Testament, the universe is about 6,000 years old.

Based on astronomical science, however, the age is closer to 13.8 billion years.

That's quite a difference between the two. So which is it?

Not being one who's delved deep into either theory, I can't say for certain which is the most correct.

At this point I'd like to clarify my position on whether or not science contradicts the Bible. The answer is an unqualified "No." It's an impossibility.

To claim the universe and everything in it disproves his existence is no different than me stating Michelangelo's paintings on the Sistine Chapel disproves his existence. The statement is pure idiocy. Therefore, it only stands to reason all of creation *must* prove God exists.

The problem arises in the *interpretation* of our scientific and biblical observations, not the observations themselves.

So back to the age of the universe. I can prove neither side. All I can tell you is I have a preference based on what I know of the character of God, and the little bits and pieces I have gleaned over my time here on earth.

Those who believe the universe is 6,000 or so years old make a fairly strong case, and those who believe it's 13.8 billion years old make an equally strong case.

Neither contradict scripture, either.

Odd? Yep.

Until we realize that even as advanced as we are in our scientific endeavors, we still have a long way to go. And since we still can't agree on all scripture, we're obviously limited there as well.

For instance, we could state that the Bible implies the universe is 6,000 years old by simply doing the math. Yet if we are to add other verses, such as Psalm 90:4 (ESV): "For a thousand years in your sight are but as yesterday when it is past, or as a watch in the night," and 2 Peter 3:8: "But do not overlook this one fact, beloved, that with the Lord one day is as a thousand years, and a thousand years as one day," the timetable we've derived from scripture may not be entirely accurate.

Those verses indicate God created time, lives outside of it, and is therefore unaffected by it.

I'm sure you can guess by now where I lean on the age of the universe.

But, again, it's a preference, not a conviction.

Why then do I lean in the direction of the universe being billions of years old?

It's quite simple: I like the idea of an infinite God who took infinite care and infinite patience to create the world and universe we now enjoy and will likely never fully understand due to its infinite complexity. It's shear immensity of both size and (possible) age only further shows the greater immensity and infinity of the God who created all of it.

However, if the moment I enter heaven and God whispers in my ear that he created the universe only 6,000 years prior, I'll smile and thank him for the clarification.

Because in the end, whether the age of the universe is thousands or billions of years old, neither change who he is.

IS ATHEISM DEAD?

(December 18, 2021)

I first heard of the book "Is Atheism Dead" by Eric Metaxas[28] about a month ago from an exclusive excerpt on The Daily Wire.[29] The excerpt (from Chapter Eighteen) described how an archeologist turned to the Bible in search of Sodom and Gomorrah. And found them after they had disappeared for many thousands of years.

I've always been a fan of science. While not a scientist by any stretch, I'm still fascinated by the natural world, its beauty and intricacies. Part of why I love to take pictures is to show people what I see. Because we're often so distracted with the busyness of life, we forget to stop and look at God's creation, even something as simple as hoarfrost collected on a tiny leaf.

While the two above paragraphs seem unrelated, hang with me a bit. It'll all make sense shortly.

Because I found the excerpt of the book so intriguing, I purchased it for my Nook the next day. But I didn't stop there. I also purchased one for a friend who loves biblical history, and one for my son who was equally intrigued (he prefers paper books over electronic). Yep, I bought three copies in a span of five days.

The author tackles not only archeological findings which prove the accuracy of scripture, he outlines in great detail how recent scientific discoveries also invariably point toward a Creator. He also does so in a way a layperson like myself can understand.

All the examples and research he goes through destroy the atheistic idea that our universe and everything in it was a thoughtless, yet happy accident.

I've always believed nature points to God, not away from him (see Romans 1:20), so I was excited to read the chapters on the Big Bang, the fine-tuning of our solar system, and the impossibility for water to do

---

[28] "Is Atheism Dead" by Eric Metaxas, Salem Books, ©2021

[29] https://www.dailywire.com/news/is-atheism-dead (must be a subscriber to read the entire article).

what it does. All of which makes life possible. If even one of those things was off by a number too small to fathom, life would not exist. At all, not even in a different form.

I found myself many times mentally (if not literally) giggling madly. So much so I had to stop reading more than once just to give my brain a moment to absorb it all.

One might say I'm guilty of "confirmation bias."[30] Perhaps, but Eric also provides enough evidence that's difficult to argue with.

Fair warning, though. While Eric writes for the layperson, it's a heady book. Four hundred pages, three parts, and thirty chapters of detailed scientific discoveries. He also pulls no punches toward those scientists and philosophers (past and present) who refuse(d) to acknowledge even the possibility our universe was indeed carefully and willfully created by *something* beyond our comprehension.

Or as I occasionally—and a bit tongue-in-cheek—call said something: The Flying Spaghetti Monster.[31]

---

[30] Reading or listening to something which confirms what we already believe while ignoring any evidence to the contrary.
[31] See entry titled "Sky Wizards and Flying Spaghetti Monsters," page 75

IS CHRISTIANITY DYING?

(December 24, 2021)

How's that for a provocative title, especially for Christmas Eve?

It comes off the heels of my previous entry "Is Atheism Dead?" and a short conversation with someone online after I posted the entry.

She had answered simply: "No."

I then asked her a few questions including why atheists seem to be more antagonistic toward Christianity than any other religion. Her answer—based on her experiences, including spending time with a group of atheists—confirmed what I already suspected. From a purely grammatical perspective, it's a well-written response. I could tell each word she chose was intentional, something the writer in me can appreciate (used with permission):

"I think the focus on 'not Jesus' is because Christianity is the most virulent in the United States, at least where I live. All of the people I met had some run in with Christian cults, not with Islam or any other. Take for instance Greek gods. Most people dismiss those as ancient fiction, so the atheists discuss them like science or history. They don't feel threatened by ancient Greek or Roman gods because there is nobody here that presses them to fire sacrifice their dinner in a temple. On the other hand, there was a Christian who came to the meetings to try and convert the atheists to his religion. These are the only examples that I know and that came out during the conversation. We didn't discuss other religions."

Her answer makes perfect sense. How can anyone honestly criticize a religion they've never been exposed to?

Nor do I think her perspective is unique.

Back in March of this year, Gallup did a study[32] revealing for the first time ever, less than 50% of the US population claim to be members of a house of worship. According to the study, it's largely due to an

---

[32] https://news.gallup.com/poll/341963/church-membership-falls-below-majority-first-time.aspx

increase of people who have no religious preference (more on that below).

Yet those who do have a religious preference are also dropping out of attending a church. Some of it appears to be generational. The older a person, the more likely they are to be a regular member/attendee. Even so, older generations are attending less or claiming no affiliation.

The fact so many churches closed over the last two years due to the thing-that-shall-not-be-named have likely caused the more precipitous drop, but the drop has been trending for decades.

So what's causing the trend?

Gallup did another study in 2017[33] which might help explain it. It boils down to what the churches themselves are doing—or not doing. According to this study, the main reasons people stay or leave a specific church are sermon content (76%), real-life applications (75%), child/teenager programs (64%), and community outreach/volunteer opportunities (59%). Lowest in importance are social activities (49%) and choir/band/music (38%).

Taking those two surveys into consideration, church attendance may be falling because their sermons, life applications, and programs for children are lacking.

Now for the anecdotal.

The church I attended for over fifteen years did all of the above necessary for a healthy church: great sermons, plenty of bible studies for all sexes and ages geared toward real-world applications, amazing community outreach, and programs for children/teens.

Until the-thing-that-shall-be-not-named hit.

I eventually left the church permanently due to fundamental disagreements with how the church responded. The details are irrelevant at this point. Suffice to say, after about a year I became one of the statistics where I claimed no church affiliation.

---

[33] https://news.gallup.com/poll/208529/sermon-content-appeals-churchgoers.aspx

Feeling a bit lost after that year, I searched for and found another church. Three things kept me coming back:

- Pastors who don't shy from or make apologies for preaching on the hard stuff. They also revere scripture; they ask the audience to stand whenever they read a passage, something I'd never seen before.
- Bible studies on a slew of subjects and for all ages and sexes.
- Youth programs. My son loves the programs so much, he looks forward to meeting every Sunday (at 8:30 am!) and Wednesday evenings. He won't even let me make excuses to not take him.

This church is also one that's growing while others are dying, making it an exception. I also live in a mid-western state where church attendance is relatively high. It's still dropping overall, just at a much slower rate.

Another reason for the attendance drops—which ties into the lack of a good message—is increasing church arguments over fundamental doctrines and even the Bible itself. Who wants to be a member of a church that can't agree over the most basic tenants of their faith, argue over what scripture does and doesn't say, and eventually splits?

Does all this mean I agree Christianity is dying?

As emphatic as the lady above was with atheism not being dead, I give an emphatic "no." Christianity isn't dying. At least not worldwide.

What's dying is the *American* church—generally speaking. Some might say it's a good thing, and for many reasons which I won't get into. This entry is already quite long, so thank you for sticking with me this far.

From my admittedly biased perspective, God is pulling his support from churches who've set aside their love of Jesus. They've instead embraced secular/societal beliefs which directly contradict scripture or for potential monetary gain (Prosperity Gospel anyone?). Or to put it more directly, he's separating the wheat from the chaff. All we can hope to remain is a remnant that holds true and will perhaps attract others who are searching for the concrete instead of the mercurial.

I always say God is a fan of paradox. I'm not alone in thinking this according to an article by Christianity Today titled, "Proof That Political Privilege is Harmful for Christianity." Subtitle: "Analysis of 166 nations suggests the biggest threat to Christian vitality is not persecution, affluence, education, or pluralism. It's state support."[34]

One quote (which, oddly enough, contradicts the above subtitle): "… some scholars have suggested the cause is rather the accumulation of wealth. Increasing prosperity, it is believed, frees people from having to look to a higher power to provide for their daily needs. In other words, there is a direct link from affluence to atheism."

We, therefore, shouldn't be surprised to see Christianity dying in western, affluent societies, yet growing by leaps in countries where it's effectively outlawed such as in China, India, and places in the Middle East.

Do I suggest we should hope for the United States government to officially outlaw Christianity and start persecuting Christians in order to see growth instead of decline? Not at all. What I hope to convey is how we need to shift our focus back to our "first love" (see Revelation 2:4-5) and worship only Jesus instead of pushing him aside in favor of the loves of this world.

If we don't, then we will see Christianity die. At least in the United States.

---

[34] https://www.christianitytoday.com/ct/2021/may-web-only/christian-persecution-political-privilege-growth-decline.html

A TOLERANT GOD?

(November 11, 2022)

I hear a lot of people, Christian and non-Christian alike, claim God is a tolerant God. He loves us regardless of who we are or what we do, because God is Love (1 John 4:8). He is merciful and constantly showers us with his grace.

To discover if the above is indeed true, I decided to do some research.

We first need to define our terms. In this case, those terms are tolerance, mercy, and grace. I focus on those three, because people seem to use those interchangeably:

Tolerance: 1. The capacity for or the practice of recognizing and respecting the beliefs or practices of others; 2. Leeway for variation from a standard; 3. The permissible deviation from a specified value of a structural dimension, often expressed as a percent.

Mercy: 1. Compassionate treatment, especially of those under one's power; clemency; 2. A disposition to be kind and forgiving; 3. Something for which to be thankful; a blessing; 4. Alleviation of distress; relief.

Grace: 1. A disposition to be generous or helpful; goodwill. 2. Mercy; clemency; 3. A favor rendered by one who need not do so; indulgence; 4. A temporary immunity or exemption; a reprieve.

I already see a difference in those definitions; they can't be interchanged so easily after all.

Since we're talking about God, though, if he was indeed tolerant as defined above, certainly we would find plenty of scriptural passages describing God thusly, wouldn't we?

So I did a word search in my Bible. I started with "tolerate" and its derivatives. Only three came up, and only two are remotely applicable:

"It is actually reported that there is sexual immorality among you, and of a kind that is not tolerated even among pagans, for a man has his father's wife."

~ 1 Corinthians 5:1 (ESV)

"But I have this against you, that you tolerate that woman, Jezebel, who calls herself a prophetess and is teaching and seducing my servants to practice sexual immorality and to eat food sacrificed to idols."

~ Revelation 2:20

We start to see God is not so tolerant after all, especially when it comes to certain sinful behavior. Nor is it a coincidence the kind of tolerance we're expected to extend—celebrate even—is for sexual sins.

What about eliminating "tolerance" and embracing "mercy" and "grace" instead? Wouldn't that result in the same thing: God accepting us of who we are, who we want and claim to be, and what we do?

My search yielded 187 results for "mercy," 37 for "merciful," and 227 for "grace." That's a lot, so I will pick two which have both terms:

"The Lord passed before him and proclaimed, 'The Lord, the Lord, a God merciful and gracious, slow to anger, and abounding in steadfast love and faithfulness, keeping steadfast love for thousands, forgiving iniquity and transgression and sin, but who will by no means clear the guilty, visiting the iniquity of the fathers on the children and the children's children, to the third and the fourth generation.'"

~ Exodus 34:6-7

"The Lord is merciful and gracious, slow to anger and abounding in steadfast love. He will not always chide, nor will he keep his anger forever. He does not deal with us according to our sins, nor repay us according to our iniquities. For as high as the heavens are above the earth, so great is his steadfast love toward those who fear him;"

~ Psalm 103:8-11

All throughout scripture, God indeed shows mercy and grace, but a caveat or two are attached as shown in the two examples above.

God *forgives* sin, meaning although he acknowledges our sinfulness, he doesn't *tolerate* or accept it and let us go on our merry way to keep sinning. In all circumstances, God requires repentance and atonement and to "go and sin no more." (John 8:11).

Scripture gives example after example of those who refused and were invariably punished and/or destroyed.

In short, tolerance accepts (and even celebrates) all things no matter how wrong or sinful, whereas grace and mercy are given when undeserved and acknowledges sin and wrongdoing.

God is indeed *intolerant* of our sins, and so should we—in ourselves as much as in others.

I don't suggest we are required to condemn others for their sin, but to offer them as much grace and mercy as God has given us—yet also with the same caveats.

PART 3: POLITICS

SINS OF THE CHRISTIAN VOTER

(December 14, 2017)

I've heard a lot of talk to the effect of: "How can you call yourself a Christian for voting for *that* candidate?"

From both Christians and non-Christians alike.

Let's use Alabama's most recent senatorial election as an example. Of the two main candidates, one is pro-life and an alleged sexual predator. The other has no sordid accusations but is staunchly pro-choice.

The Christian faces a hard choice: Vote for the alleged predator who believes life at all stages deserves protection, or the second candidate who thinks abortion should be legal up until birth but was never accused of preying on young women.

This Christian voter needs to decide which sins the candidates have committed are the most and least egregious.

The Christian can also not vote or write in a better candidate. Perhaps a third-party choice if one is listed.

That's not the end of the struggle, however. Once the choice is made, the Christian has to decide to never reveal the choice or openly support said chosen candidate.

This is a difficult one. By staying silent when unfair criticism of chosen candidate arises, the Christian can continue to remain silent or risk being counted as (and accused of) supporting either sexual assault or infanticide.

Most Christians expect criticism from the worldly no matter what they do. After all, the world hated Jesus first (see John 15:18).

What Christians don't expect is to hear such vitriolic criticism from fellow Christians. Aren't they all members of the body of Christ, united in a common cause and inseparable?

Here's how I see it:

Government is a secular institution. Any person we vote for is a fallible, sinful human being, and each seeks to occupy an office equally secular in nature. It's neither a religious nor spiritual occupation. Therefore, our standards shouldn't be the same as voting for a new pastor or priest. The qualifications and expectations are too different.

Aside: Do we all want good, moral people to lead us? Absolutely! Still, even moral people are flawed, so no matter how good they appear, they are still sinful (that and what society considers moral and immoral are in constant flux). Voters, Christian and otherwise, are too often faced with deciding which candidate holds to their own worldview the closest—the least of evils. Or perhaps not vote at all and let the chips fall where they may.

What concerns me is how willing so many Christians are to judge, condemn, and divide over political lines.

Paul warned us against divisions in 1 Corinthians 1:10-17, and how we're all parts of a single body with different roles to fulfill in 1 Corinthians 12.

When we allow the world generally—and politics specifically—to divide us, the Body falters, and we lose both sight and effectiveness of our mandate to uplift others and spread the Good News. Those we seek to save instead laugh at us. Because of our petty and public arguments and the constant finger-pointing, we deserve to be mocked.

Instead of condemning the political choices others make, let God judge the heart and intent of the voter, because the rest of us are far from qualified.

In other words, watch for those planks instead of scrounging around for specks (Matthew 7:5).

A PIXELATED VIEW

(January 9, 2018)

Have you ever zoomed into a digital photo so close all you see is a bunch of fuzzy, colored squares? If someone were to walk by the computer screen, they'd never guess what the photo shows, or that it's even a photograph.

Only after zooming out does the picture become clear.

I think politics does the same thing, especially if we spend so much time delving into it, and from a single point of view. For instance, I mention President Donald Trump and some people react with a visceral loathing while others cheer "MAGA!"[35]

Polar opposite reactions over the same human being.

For the last few months, I've grown tired of politics. Anyone with a phone or computer uses their electronic soapbox to opine and usually with either a left or right point of view. It's tiresome and predictable.

As one also armed with multiple electronic devices, I am tempted to follow only those who fall into the same political spectrum as me. After all, why follow those with whom I disagree when all their words do is make me angry and frustrated?

Still, I refuse to give in to the temptation, and the answer is simple: I don't like pixelated photographs. They look choppy, out of focus, little to no contrast to make the subject pop, too few colors, and the details are non-existent. Uninteresting. Boring.

Another word people use to describe looking at things from a single point of view is "myopic." It means "lacking imagination, foresight, or intellectual insight." Isn't that a great word? And so accurate!

Since I never want to be accused of having no intellectual insight, I've decided to zoom out and attempt to see the world as a whole in all its shadows, sixteen-million-plus colors, contrast, depth, and richness.

---

[35] Donald Trump's campaign slogan meaning "Make America Great Again."

I resolve to push my political biases behind me. When I see a post or article I'll likely disagree with, still I read it, gritted teeth and involuntary shakes of the head notwithstanding.

In doing so I've stumbled on a few gems of wisdom. Did I agree with everything I read? Not at all. Sometimes as little as ten percent. But still, one piece of new knowledge or wisdom out of ten is one more than I had before.

The impetus of this entry comes from comments made on a political website about commentator, Ben Shapiro. The comments were particularly vicious for the simple reason he was critical of Donald Trump during the presidential primaries—a so-called "Never Trumper." I often listen to his podcast, and while he's still critical of Trump, he also gives him credit when it's due. The funny part is, the commenters refuse to give Shapiro credit when it's due. Since I know their political leanings, they would find more in common with Shapiro than not. Based on their responses when I tried to defend him, however, they are suffering from their own myopathy. Or to stick with my original analogy, they prefer to stare at pixelated photographs.

It's a shame, really, because we are so much more than our labels and opinions.

Yet too many of us aren't willing to step back from staring at a smattering of pixels to get a larger and deeper understanding of the entire picture.

CARBON COPY CHRISTIANS

(December 24, 2018)

How do you like my alliteration, there?

Yesterday someone posted this on Twitter: "To the 'Christians' who gave money for a GoFundMe to build Trump's Wall, there are children & veterans without shoes, sick people without healthcare, a city without drinking water, and immigrants fleeing from certain death. Please reevaluate your Christian values and try again!"

I responded thusly: "Do you have proof that Christians who donated for the wall don't also help children, veterans, the sick, etc.? If not, then your assumption is false. Christians can do more than one thing and donate to more than one cause, you know."

This isn't about the wall or politics, but how some perceive Christians in general. They seem to think we're all monochromatic in our beliefs and actions. Truth is, I know many Christians who:

Believe God condemns slavery;

Believe God approves of or condones slavery;

Believe God condones the abuse of women and children;

Believe God both condemns and expects punishment of all abusers;

Believe Jesus was a pacifist;

Believe Jesus was a warrior;

Believe God would be for gun control and all guns should be banned;

Believe God would not expect people to give up their ability to protect themselves with firearms or other weaponry;

Donate to liberal causes;

Donate to conservative causes;

Vote Democrat;

Vote Republican;

Want a border wall;

Don't want a border wall;

Want bigger government;

Want smaller government;

Want lower taxes;

Want higher taxes;

And the list goes on.

People insulting Christians, or non-Christians telling Christians how they should act is a pet peeve of mine. I can't tell a Jew, Buddhist, or Muslim how to act or worship, because I don't know enough about their religion to make that call. Now, if they do something illegal or harmful to others (Christian and non-Christian alike), then yes, I will shamelessly point fingers. Not as far as how someone decides to spend their time or money, however, because it's none of my business. In the end it's between them and God.

Still, although it bugs me, I don't get as upset as I used to, because someone reminded me of a verse where Jesus said, "If the world hates you, know that it has hated me before it hated you." (John 15:18).

Therefore, I should be more surprised when people (non-Christians especially) express love and admiration for Christians.

A sidetrack here: You might wonder how people within a single religion could have so many opposing beliefs. One reason is we're all individuals with different backgrounds, experiences, and therefore points of view. Because the Bible is so big written by many authors and with many messages and stories, to approach it with our own, colored view, to see what we want to see and be blind to the rest is easy. Especially when those parts seem to contradict each other.

I'm reading "The Rational Bible: Exodus" by Dennis Prager[36]. He said (paraphrased) that God always leaves us room for doubt, including doubt in him and whether or not he even exists. Now why would he do that? He's God, after all. Couldn't he reveal himself to everyone in a single moment so no one could deny his existence? Sure, but he also wants to be *chosen*, just as we prefer to be chosen and having choices—whatever those choices may be.

No one doubts the Sun gives heat, or that winter is cold, and summer is warm. Why? Because they're obvious based on mere observation. They're undeniable and therefore require no faith.

---

[36] "The Rational Bible: Exodus" by Dennis Prager, Regnery Faith, ©2018

God wants to be sought after, and yes, expects to be doubted. Part of it is because he loves it when we ask him questions, to seek truth and understanding. Doubt spurs us to ask those questions. No questions can be asked if we already know all the answers. Mystery is a fabulous thing because of the joy of discovery.

Someone once asked Dennis Prager why he's a Jew and not Muslim. He said (again, paraphrased), "Because Israel means to struggle or wrestle with God whereas Islam means to submit. I prefer to wrestle with God than submit."

So do I. Sure, God always wins in the end—even if he does cheat sometimes. Just ask Jacob (Genesis 32:22-32). I have grown more in my faith by wrestling with God than simply submitting to him. Why? Because I gain more understanding of who God is and why he does what he does after that struggle.

Don't we all want people to ask us questions, to be noticed, believed, and understood?

PART 4: FAITH

THE ADVANTAGE OF GROWING UP GODLESS

(November 23, 2015)

A friend of mine recently wrote of her experiences growing up in a "Christian" home where her parents taught the only way to heaven was to act and think a certain way. Whenever she and her siblings failed to meet that standard, they were punished and told they would burn in Hell. Forgiveness could not be attained by merely asking for it; they had to prove themselves worthy of it. She also described how the cruelty of her family's teachings nearly forced her to give up faith in God.

Her experiences were so foreign to me, yet it still broke my heart.

Every child experiences some form of great pain, pain that never goes away even into adulthood. It forms our long-term fears and can even determine our day-to-day interactions. Letting go of those memories is almost impossible. The pain becomes almost a part of our DNA, and it surfaces when we're unsure, scared, or hurting. How can we keep our near-instinctual pain in the past so it doesn't affect our present or determine our future?

About ten years ago I decided to write in my first blog every painful memory I carried with me. I can't tell you how cathartic it was. For whatever reason, writing it down and sharing with others made them less painful.

They no longer exerted power over me.

The one pain I never had to deal with is the pain of religion—or at least misinterpreted religion which paints God as cruel, angry, and unforgiving. My parents rarely discussed God. Since they didn't believe in him, they had no reason to talk about him. I remember my mom was a bit hostile when it came to organized religion, though. I don't know why, but I'm willing to bet she was burned by it much like my friend above.

While my mom didn't go into any tirades about religion, I knew enough that my rebellion as a teenager was to attend church. No lie.

I consider myself lucky. The church I first attended focused on Jesus—who he was (and is)—and God's immeasurable love for us.

Growing up in a home without God, I developed no pre-conceived notions of an angry, vengeful, and spiteful God, let alone a loving one. When I started my search for God, I was, and am, able to see him with clearer eyes and mind. A clean slate if you will.

One day some parents brought their children to Jesus so he could touch and bless them. But the disciples scolded the parents for bothering him. When Jesus saw what was happening, he was angry with his disciples. He said to them, "Let the children come to me. Don't stop them! For the Kingdom of God belongs to those who are like these children. I tell you the truth, anyone who doesn't receive the Kingdom of God like a child will never enter it." Then he took the children in his arms and placed his hands on their heads and blessed them.

~ Mark 10:13-15 (NLT)

That's the key, I think. Children are innocent. They haven't learned how to distrust. They believe anything is possible, and they are worthy of being loved, no matter what.

Jesus calls us to be like those children.

Since I started my own spiritual journey with Jesus, I have learned that God does not accuse me but instead shows me mercy when I do wrong, comforts me when I hurt, cheers for me when I succeed, and shows me a better way when I've strayed.

My biggest prayer is so everyone could see God in a similar way. To release any past toxins (religious or otherwise) and to consider the idea of a loving God instead of an angry one. And most of all, for everyone to relegate past pains to the past and embrace the joys of today.

To be children once again.

I can appreciate how difficult that is for some, especially those who have been damaged during their formative years, but Jesus is all about making the impossible possible.

SKY WIZARDS AND FLYING SPAGHETTI MONSTERS

(September 17, 2017)

I have a few friends who are not only atheists but are outright hostile to any belief in a higher power.

More than once they've described God as a "Sky Wizard," or "Flying Spaghetti Monster." Even as a Christian, I find those descriptions humorous even though they're designed to insult. The latter one is my favorite.

To a person who doesn't believe God exists, to pray to a non-existent entity is pure foolishness. It gives an individual's power away, and—according to them—is used as an excuse to not act so they can be their own answer to prayer.

For instance, someone might pray for healing. The atheist assumes that by praying, the person isn't seeking medical help. And if they are healed, that person should be giving the doctors credit, not some imagined creature who lives in the sky.

I've seen people complain about praying for those harmed by the latest hurricanes and western state forest fires. They assume those who pray aren't doing anything else. They accuse them of thinking God is going to wave his magic wand and fix everything, and those praying don't have to do anything themselves to help.

First off, that's false, because I know many who prayed have also sent money, goods, and even gone down there to help. So, yes, we are often our own answers to prayer.

I and many others have also seen miracles which can't be explained by science, but that's an entry for another time.

And what about the times God doesn't seem to answer our prayers? Doesn't that alone prove he can't exist?

God is not Santa Claus, nor is he a genie. He knows what's best for us a lot more than we do. I have prayed for many things when God said no, and in looking back, I'm so glad he did. I could give plenty of examples, but that would make this entry far too long.

Prayer is also not just about what we receive, whether it'd be our finances or our health. Prayer changes us. We're open to not only the possibilities, but it's also our best way of communicating with God and building a relationship with him. Every relationship we've ever had, and ever will have, changes us. Sometimes for good, sometimes not. With God, however, it's always for our good, even if we sometimes hate him for it. For a time. Or maybe that's just me...

Wouldn't you get annoyed if the only time a person came around was to ask for something? Pretty soon, you wouldn't answer the door anymore. But if that person also tried to build a relationship with you, not ask for something in return every time, and tended to be generous themselves, then you'd be more inclined to help when they're in need. God isn't much different.

All of this, however, will fall on deaf ears to those who refuse to believe God exists, let alone that he cares enough to want to build a relationship with us. They first must *consider* the possibility before it *becomes* a possibility.

For example, people used to believe the world was flat. Based on their experience such as looking at the horizon, it's flat. Therefore, the earth is flat.

Yet some considered the possibility that the world was round and then set out to prove it. Christopher Columbus is the most obvious example. For him, the idea—the possibility—came before he could set sail to seek out proof.

That's how faith started for all of us believers in God, aka The Flying Spaghetti Monster.

MY BEAUTIFUL CRUTCH

(September 28, 2017)

I'm attending an interesting Bible study on Wednesdays at my church called Skeptics where we talk about controversial subjects relating to God and religion.

Atheism came up in the conversation last night, and someone said how an atheist friend once told him, "People use religion as a crutch."

I've heard that before, too. Then it occurred to me. Yes, religion—faith—is a crutch.

And that's a good thing.

Would we tell someone with a broken leg to not use crutches to get around, or a paraplegic to not use his/her wheelchair? That would not only be idiotic but insulting. Perhaps even cruel.

Just as anyone injured or handicapped can't move around and be independent without their physical aids, people of faith can't function at their best—be independent—without depending on God.

It seems counter-intuitive, doesn't it? How does one live independently while depending on God?

Part of faith in God is admitting we're weak. We don't have all the answers, and we can't control everything—sometimes not even ourselves. That's a tough one to admit, because especially here in the States, we are taught that we can control our destiny. We have so many choices. For example, we can still (for the most part) decide who we marry, who we associate with, schools, colleges, and career choices.

Yet we can't control when we catch a cold, if we'll contract a fatal disease, if someone commits a crime against us, nature's wrath, when our loved ones pass, when a friend breaks a trust, the list is near infinite.

Faith teaches that control is an illusion. Nor does control bring us hope, joy, or courage. Faith in God and the decision to depend on him and his wisdom instead of our flawed, human understanding is what brings us all those things and more.

Without my faith I wouldn't have had the courage to broach a difficult subject which resulted in the birth of our son (long story, that).

Without depending on God, I wouldn't have the courage to write, let alone share it with anyone.

So, yes, God is my crutch, and I shout it proudly.

He's my unfailing, beautiful crutch.

BELIEVE OR ELSE—UNTIL YOU LEAVE THE HOUSE

(April 27, 2018)

I overheard a boy say, "I have to believe in God until I turn eighteen or when I move out. Then I can believe whatever I want."

I found that a little concerning. It almost sounded as though faith was being forced on him, and how he looked forward to not believing in God later in life.

Faith should never be forced on anyone.

Some could argue Christians believe just that. Even Jesus said those who don't believe in him will die (John 3:16-20 and John 8:24). History abounds of instances where churches killed or imprisoned those who refused to convert.

I won't argue church history except to say they got it wrong. Jesus never told anyone to force others to believe; he merely stated what will happen to those who refuse (see Matthew 13:41-42 & 49-50).

We are all still free to choose as long as we first consider the consequences of that choice.

Nor can anyone force someone to believe anything anyway. Sure, we can say we believe in God to appease others, but we are fabulous liars. We, in fact, more often than not tend to hide what's true in our heart—both good and bad.

Jesus, however, knows what's in our heart regardless. Sure, scripture says we must confess with our mouth that Jesus is Lord (Romans 10:9), but we must accept it as truth in our heart first.

Jesus will always know the difference even when those around us don't:

"These people honor me with their lips, but their hearts are far from me."

~ Matthew 15:8 & Isaiah 29:13 (NLT)

I also had to ask a question of myself. Am I forcing my own son to believe in Jesus? After all, I take him with me to church twice a week, he goes to a Christian school, I pray with him every night, and I keep my car radio on a Christian station.

Yet I never once said, "Believe or else."

Exposing and even immersing my son in my faith is showing him how important Jesus is. At the same time, I try to encourage him to ask questions, even (especially) the hard questions. Still, I know that no matter how much I encourage him to believe, the choice will always be his—the whole leading the horse to water stuff.

We should encourage and not threaten when it comes to faith. Children most of all. They all rebel in one form or another, and if we present our faith as tyrannical and unattractive, they will run away from it the first chance they get—perhaps permanently.

I'll leave you with these:

Children, obey your parents because you belong to the Lord, for this is the right thing to do.
"Honor your father and mother." This is the first commandment with a promise: If you honor your father and mother, "things will go well for you, and you will have a long life on the earth."
Fathers, do not provoke your children to anger by the way you treat them. Rather, bring them up with the discipline and instruction that comes from the Lord.
~ Ephesians 6:1-4

So commit yourselves wholeheartedly to these words of mine. Tie them to your hands and wear them on your forehead as reminders. Teach them to your children. Talk about them when you are at home and when you are on the road, when you are going to bed and when you are getting up.
~ Deuteronomy 11:18-19

Direct your children onto the right path, and when they are older, they will not leave it.
~ Proverbs 22:6

DEFEND YOURSELF!

(January 11, 2019)

"I learned a long time ago that anything worth doing is worth defending."

~ Mike Rowe

Does God call us to follow him blindly and without question?

Some like to accuse Christians of being blind sheep, ready to dive off a cliff simply because God said so. I've heard some Christians accuse others that to doubt and question is a lack of trust and faith in God—and could even be considered blasphemous (I was told this once as a teenager when I said God makes me angry sometimes).

In a previous entry called "Carbon Copy Christians," I talked about how God appreciates when we doubt. A friend commented thusly (in part), "Though a Christian may from time struggle with the no fear part of our faith, I believe when we still follow God's word despite that fear, that God rejoices in our faith, love for him. So submit to His Word!"

To which I respond:

I'm not suggesting God doesn't rejoice in our faith. Of course he does! Nor does doubt mean we love God less. All I'm saying is God understands and even expects us to doubt. Having doubts is part of who we are in this world. Nor do I recall him ever saying we should never ask him questions or to never get angry at or frustrated with him. Acting out in that anger is a bit different. A good example is when God told Moses he couldn't enter the promised land because he acted out in anger and as such didn't give God proper credit (see Numbers 20).

As if we could hide our doubts from him anyway.

Doubt isn't always a bad thing, as long as we go to him with those doubts.

Moses argued with God, as did Abraham (which saved Lot and his family). David and Job had doubts. Lots of doubts! Jonah tried to run away and got angry with God when Nineveh repented. Naomi (from the book of Ruth) believed God had abandoned her. Peter argued with Jesus, Thomas doubted him, and Paul worked against him.

So what does all that have to do with defending oneself as the title suggests?

When we struggle and doubt—and as long as we turn to God with those struggles and doubts—he teaches us where we have fallen short or are mistaken in our assumptions. When we learn through those doubts and struggles, we grow stronger in our faith and can better defend that faith.

God often compares us to sheep, because sheep are stupid creatures. They will literally jump off a cliff following other sheep, never realizing the danger until it's too late. That does not mean, however, God wants us to remain like sheep. He wants us to be able to defend our faith to those who also question and struggle (including ourselves).

Proverbs 2:1-5 (ESV) says:

"My son, if you receive my words and treasure up my commandments with you, making your ear attentive to wisdom and inclining your heart to understanding; yes, if you call out for insight and raise your voice for understanding, if you seek it like silver and search for it as for hidden treasures, then you will understand the fear of the Lord and find the knowledge of God."

Other such examples of the importance of seeking God and his wisdom and defending our faith:

"All Scripture is breathed out by God and profitable for teaching, for reproof, for correction, and for training in righteousness, that the man of God may be complete, equipped for every good work."

~ 2 Timothy 3:16-17

"but in your hearts honor Christ the Lord as holy, always being prepared to make a defense to anyone who asks you for a reason for the hope that is in you; yet do it with gentleness and respect,"

~ 1 Peter 3:15

"We destroy arguments and every lofty opinion raised against the knowledge of God, and take every thought captive to obey Christ,"
~ 2 Corinthians 10:5

"He must hold firm to the trustworthy word as taught, so that he may be able to give instruction in sound doctrine and also to rebuke those who contradict it."
~ Titus 1:9

In short, yes, we need to submit to God and his word, but by submitting without question or not attempting to overcome our doubts, we can neither grow, understand, nor defend our faith.

ABOUT WHAT'S NOT SAID

(October 14, 2019)

I'm reading Leviticus which is basically a manual of instruction for the Levites—the tribe of Hebrew priests.

A lot of it is repetition as far as animal sacrifices, when someone is considered "unclean," and how to be cleansed. Some of it seems harsh, especially how women are treated with regard to their menstrual cycle and how long they had to be sequestered after they gave birth. The time of sequestration also varied depending on whether they gave birth to a boy or a girl.

I have to remember that was a very different time, and they didn't know as much about hygiene as we do—much of which we take for granted today.

But I digress.

The Israelites, before the Exodus, were surrounded by people who worshiped false gods. Many of them made human as well as animal sacrifice.

Why God felt it wise to continue the animal sacrifice I can't answer, but I trust his reasoning was both important and logical for the Hebrews at that time.

Again, I digress.

Why did people sacrifice to their gods? What's the first thing you think of?

For me, in stories I've read and movies I've seen, people sacrificed to their gods in order to find some kind of favor.

In Leviticus 8, God requires sacrifices for forgiveness or thanksgiving—and animal sacrifice only. No human sacrifice. Another stark difference with their neighbors. Leviticus says nothing about sacrifices in order to receive anything else such as wealth, status, children, or long life. I can't help but wonder if that's on purpose, as another means to set the Israelites apart from their neighbors, and to show God can neither be bought nor bribed.

It occurred to me then that sometimes what's not said is just as important as what is said.

FEWER RULES, HIGHER STANDARDS

(October 21, 2019)

More on Leviticus (sort of).

Along with describing the rules of animal sacrifice, Leviticus shows just how much the Israelites were required to do with regard to cleanliness, disease diagnosis and control of its spread, and also criminal punishment (see Leviticus 24:17-22).

Then Jesus comes along and turns much of that around. We are no longer required to make animal sacrifices to atone for our sins. Jesus became that perfect and eternal sacrifice, so it's no longer necessary. That's not to say we don't have to ask for forgiveness or atone for our sins in other ways, however. If anything, what God requires for forgiveness is a bit more difficult. Instead of sacrificing an animal, we have to sacrifice our pride. Ourselves. It's a sacrifice of the mind and heart that requires (gasp!) humility.

Aside: Does that mean we give up who we are and become mindless automatons? Not remotely! God wants us to continually seek him out, ask questions, sometimes, yes, even struggle with him when we're angry or frustrated. That's how relationships work sometimes. What we must never give up, however, is trust. Although we may not understand what God does or doesn't do, we have to trust he knows what he's doing and will always have our best and eternal interests in mind.

Many of the laws laid out in Exodus and in Leviticus include various punishments based on a person's actions such as murder, thievery, adultery, etc.

While Jesus told us to forgive other people's sins (accepting the legal consequences of those sins, whether they be murder, stealing, and the like is a different conversation), he also changed the standards.

No longer are we guilty of murder if we literally murder someone; we are guilty of murder when we hate someone. We're no longer guilty of adultery if we sleep with someone other than our spouse; we commit adultery when we lust after someone else's spouse.

Not only did he raise the standards, they're God's way of telling us yet again (because he also states this many times in the Old Testament; the New Testament is just a bit more emphatic about it) that sin always starts in the heart, not when we commit the act. If we refuse to entertain sinful behavior in our heart and mind, we can't act on them.

"And the peace of God, which surpasses all understanding, will guard your hearts and your minds in Christ Jesus.
"Finally, brothers, whatever is true, whatever is honorable, whatever is just, whatever is pure, whatever is lovely, whatever is commendable, if there is any excellence, if there is anything worthy of praise, think about these things. What you have learned and received and heard and seen in me—practice these things, and the God of peace will be with you."
~ Philippians 4:7-9 (ESV)

A HARSH REBUKE

(May 31, 2020)

"But turning and seeing his disciples, he rebuked Peter and said, 'Get behind me Satan! For you are not setting your mind on the things of God, but on the things of man.'"

~ Mark 8:33 (ESV)

I often wonder what Jesus felt at that moment. Knowing his life would soon end, was Satan tempting him to stay? Was the rebuke as much for himself as for Peter?

Curiosity aside, when God does something which goes contrary to everything I want or think I need, I argue with him. I beg him to change his mind. Intellectually I know God will always do what's best, and I will never, ever win an argument against him. Still, I continue to try. He doesn't rebuke me as harshly as Jesus did Peter, but I wonder if perhaps he should.

Or maybe God doesn't need to rebuke me, but me who needs to rebuke myself and Satan for muddling my heart and my mind from the things of God.

It's easy to do. We are finite creatures on this earth. We have our daily struggles and distractions that to focus on God's long, eternal view can be near impossible. We lose sight of our trust and faith and focus instead on our worries, our doubts, or our pride. Perhaps a combination of all three. We must remember that even when we get lost, God never does, and he never loses sight of us or what he wants to accomplish through us.

When we feel lost, we should speak Jesus' own words: "Get behind me Satan, for my mind will not be set on the things of man, but on the things of God."

AN UPSIDE-DOWN WORLD

(August 6, 2020)

The seven deadly sins are: pride, greed, lust, envy, gluttony, wrath, and sloth[37].

Contrast those with the seven corresponding virtues: humility, charity, chastity, gratitude, temperance, patience, and diligence.

Whenever I see a "celebrate [specific] pride month" declaration (and they seem to get more numerous every year), I cringe. I have to fight my own pride so it doesn't get the best of me, because I know firsthand the damage it can do.

Isaiah warns us in 5:20 (ESV):

"Woe to those who call evil good and good evil, who put darkness for light and light for darkness, who put bitter for sweet and sweet for bitter!"

He continues in verse 21 with:

"Woe to those who are wise in their own eyes, and shrewd in their own sight!"

The rest of the chapter goes on with what the Lord of Hosts will do to those who reject him and his law.

Similar warnings are repeated in 2 Timothy 3:1-4:

"But understand this, that in the last days there will come times of difficulty. For people will be lovers of self, lovers of money, proud, arrogant, abusive, disobedient to their parents, ungrateful, unholy, heartless, unappeasable, slanderous, without self-control, brutal, not

---

[37] According to Encyclopedia Britannica, the list was "First enumerated by Pope Gregory I in the 6th century and elaborated in the 13th century by St. Thomas Aquinas…" (https://www.britannica.com/topic/seven-deadly-sins)

I wouldn't be surprised if the seven deadly sins originated from those verses.

People today are not only embracing pride, gluttony, sloth, etc., they're vilifying anyone who embraces the seven virtues such as humility, chastity, and diligence.

To get angry, scared, or depressed while watching God's warnings unfold before our eyes is easy. I've been figuratively screaming at the sky like Grandpa Simpson for months now, because my own warnings seem to make little difference. The only ones who hear are those who already agree.

I often wonder why I keep trying to plant seeds on what is obviously infertile ground.

I can already hear the thoughts of some of you. You're itching to respond, to tell me what I appear to be missing:

God himself. The power of the Holy Spirit working in our hearts and in the world. Yes, we are being warned, and things do appear to be falling apart. Yet God himself is not deterred, broken, or swayed, so neither should we be deterred, broken, or swayed. The ground may look hard and infertile, but it could merely be parched, awaiting us to toss out a few seeds so God's Spirit can sprinkle a little rain, allowing those seeds to take root and grow.

Yes, we live in an upside-down world, but God is still working, diligently and without pause—even if we don't often see the results.

He still expects us to do our part, though. Not by focusing on the seven deadly sins so much as making sure we're living by the seven virtues.

CHOOSING FEAR

(October 22, 2020)

Is fear a choice? I've been asking this question of myself lately.

When my son was a bit younger, I allowed him to do things which could have hurt him: climbing trees, crawling up steep riverbanks, yes even using knives and matches after I showed him how to properly and safely use both. Nor did I ever leave his side when he did.

Some have asked me why, and the answer is simple. If he scrapes a knee, cuts or burns himself, he'll quickly learn not to do it again. Because pain is the best teacher out there. More so than his mom constantly screaming, "Don't do that; you'll hurt yourself!"

Almost all mothers learn early on that children don't always listen to motherly warnings, and they eventually push against her natural desire to protect them from harm.

The line between teaching children prudence and thoughtfulness when it comes to taking risks or teaching them to be *afraid* of taking risks is fine indeed.

Because, as pain is a powerful teacher, fear is a powerful motivator. Healthy fear can prevent us from taking too big of a risk resulting in injury or death, or at least make us pause before we leap. Again, it's a fine line, and everyone's line is different. You'll never see me parachute out of an airplane, but invite me on a fighter jet, I'm there!

Then there's another, unrelenting fear which sticks with us day after day. All one has to do is look around to know we are drowning in it: fear of who'll be elected; fear of losing our liberties (and in some instances, being allowed to keep them); fear of deadly disease; fear of natural (and unnatural) disasters. The list is endless.

Sometimes that fear can motivate us to work against any of the above such as voting, running for office or campaigning for those of like mind, living healthy to strengthen the body, and preparing for natural and unnatural disasters. Again the list is endless. Being proactive is key in eliminating those fears.

While fear can be a good thing, it can also hinder and cause us real damage. Unhealthy fear tends to overwhelm, not motivate. When it grabs hold, we isolate ourselves, lose trust in the people and world around us, and in the end we quit living, because that fear too often leads to loneliness and despair.

As usual, I must turn to scripture. What does God say about being afraid, and is it really a choice?

And as usual, because fear is universal and affects us in so many negative ways, the Bible is filled with verses about it. Since this entry is getting a bit long, I will share only three. You should see a common thread in all of them:

"Fear not, for I am with you; be not dismayed, for I am your God; I will strengthen you, I will help you, I will uphold you with my righteous hand."

~ Isaiah 41:10 (ESV)

"For God gave us a spirit not of fear but of power love and self-control."

~ 2 Timothy 1:7

"Do not be anxious about anything, but in everything by prayer and supplication with thanksgiving let your requests be made known to God. And the peace of God, which surpasses all understanding, will guard your hearts and your minds in Christ Jesus."

~ Philippians 4:6-7

All three (and every other verse I searched for) stressed the importance of depending on God—that only he can give us the strength and means to rise above our fears.

By wallowing in fear, we are in effect saying God cannot be trusted or depended upon to protect us. The last verse in particular shows us what we can do.

It's not easy, though. Far from it. It takes conscious, intentional effort. Sometimes daily, if not a minute-by-minute effort through constant, thankful prayer and supplication.

Yet it's never without reward such as God's peace, and protection of our heart and mind. When we fill our heart and mind with God and his promises, there's no room left for fear.

BOWING TO NEBUCHADNEZZAR

(November 14, 2020)

I ran into a friend this morning and we got to chatting. At one point she mentioned the book of Daniel, and it reminded me of something I wrote back in 2015. After reading through it again, it seems even more applicable today and worth a repeat:

Yesterday a friend and I talked on Facebook about all the horrible things going on in the world. She commented, "Seriously I do wonder if we're now living in the end times. The world is in a dreadful state and it is just getting worse."

To which I responded:

I used to think that, but—at least from what I read—globally, before and during WWII things, were a lot worse.

Some days I wonder why God is still waiting and wish he'd just end it already. Other days I'm grateful he's not, because it gives everyone more opportunities to both spread and understand the truth.

I feel selfish by wanting it to end, because it's coming from a place of fear in that I don't want to see my nation fall or for my good life to end. I have to constantly remind myself that God is still in control. Even if hardships I can't even imagine are to come, I know eternity with God awaits me.

I just hope I continue to have the wherewithal to show God's love to others, but I sometimes (often) wonder why I bother since so many hearts are hardened against him.

At least that's how it seems. I could easily be wrong about that. I'll never know when my words or deeds will influence someone the right way. Jesus didn't give up; God hasn't given up. Nor should I, because then I am no good to him or those who need him.

I've heard a few people express concern that Christians are about to enter an era of persecution in Western countries, including the United States.

I often wonder the same thing, especially recently. But then I thought, are trials and persecutions a bad thing—at least as far as the Kingdom of God is concerned?

In all instances when people or governments tried to eliminate Christianity, it instead resulted in explosive growth. Today, the highest percentage of Christian expansion is occurring in China and other oppressive regimes where it's illegal. Our country is also experiencing revival in spite of state and local governments shutting down or restraining churches (or perhaps because of it?).

To stand with the faithless when they're standing is easy. Not so much when they all sit down. That's when the faithful are noticed. To be singled out and take the risk of being vilified at best—killed at worst can be terrifying.

That doesn't mean we should sit down, however. When the faithless sit down is the exact moment when we must stand up taller. If we don't, we show the world we have fallen prey to our own fears; we prove our own faithlessness and even distrust of God's promises.

The book of Daniel describes when Nebuchadnezzar built his ninety-foot-tall golden statue. All people from every nation were required to bow down to worship it. Shadrach, Meshach and Abednego refused. They stood up when everyone else bowed. The king noticed and demanded they be thrown into a fiery furnace. Because of their faithfulness, the fires didn't touch them, and the king and all his men bowed down to worship God.

Sure, their faith led them into the furnace, but it also led them right back out again.

I like to say God loves paradox. He uses our weaknesses to show his strength. He uses the darkest moments in our lives to shine the light of his grace, his love, and his promises.

He uses the world's attempt to kill Christianity in order to further his Kingdom.

We must be part of that, otherwise our own faith is meaningless.

Therefore, do not be afraid of any trials and tribulations, now or in the future. Don't fret about governments' attempts at restraining or destroying the Church or our faith. Welcome them, because people will see Jesus most clearly during those times. Our mortal lives and daily comforts should be the smallest price we have to pay to help accomplish it.

FORCING GRATITUDE

(November 25, 2020)

Interesting title, don't you think? Is it even possible? Can gratitude really be forced?

For someone to attempt to force others to be grateful, the answer is no. One can *act* grateful for fear of certain consequences, but in their heart and mind, I'll wager they'd be far from grateful. I'd even bet they'd be angry and resentful.

I'll admit I'm of the latter. With Thanksgiving[38] just around the corner, while no one is forcing me to be grateful (as such), I am having a difficult time convincing myself I should be. The whole reason behind the holiday is to express our thanksgiving and gratitude to God for all our blessings.

And I should. Intellectually, I know that. My heart, however, is stubborn. It prefers to mope. To be resentful and keep count of all my losses, frustrations, and failures. Even pointing out how many have lost more than me isn't enough to pull my heart out of its malaise.

I know I'm not alone. No one is enjoying the current upheaval—except politicians, bureaucrats, and tech companies—the loss of liberties, and the general isolation from friends and family. The latter is especially difficult to accept right now considering Thanksgiving has always been about gathering and sharing in the year's blessings.

We can't celebrate that one cornerstone of the holiday this year whether due to family members choosing not to or by government edict. What, then, is the purpose of celebrating it now when it's largely stripped of its meaning?

I know what some of you are thinking: I can still celebrate with my immediate family. I can still celebrate with others online. I can still count my many other blessings—for which I am self-aware and honest enough to know they're innumerable.

---

[38] This entry was also written during the height of the so-called COVID-19 pandemic when many governments shut everything down, including holidays such as Thanksgiving and Christmas.

Yet ignoring what my heart is telling me is not a solution. It's pulling the wool over my own eyes.

Unless someone can show me different, no scripture exists that states we must ignore our griefs. And that's what I'm feeling: grief over losing my country; grief over losing my God-given liberties; grief over my forced isolation; and grief of the certainty it'll only get worse.

While God doesn't demand we never grieve or ignore it, he expects us not to wallow in it, and he always provides ways to rise above it. I'll admit when I searched for relevant scriptures, I was inundated with so many possibilities, how could I possibly narrow it down?

I concentrated on Psalms because David so often wrote about his own doubts, struggles, and grief:

"Weeping may remain for a night, but rejoicing comes in the morning."
~ Psalm 30:5a (NIV)

"The righteous cry out, and the Lord hears them; he delivers them from all their troubles. The Lord is close to the brokenhearted and saves those who are crushed in spirit."
~Psalm 34:17-18

"Be still and know that I am God."
~ Psalm 46:10

"He heals the brokenhearted and binds up their wounds."
~ Psalm 147:3

In short, no matter how much we grieve, God is there to lift us up. We just need to take a moment, be still, listen, and healing will come. As long as we believe he will, that is.

While gratitude can't be forced, deciding to be grateful is certainly in our best interest.

Otherwise all we have to hope for is despair.

SEEK THEE FIRST

(January 19, 2021)

Every Monday evening, I participate in an hour-long Twitter chat using the hashtag "healthyfaith." One person hosts and asks ten questions either about a certain subject or a particular chapter/verse of the Bible.

Last night's was about meditation and how Christians should view/practice meditation vs how the world views/practices it.

The short version is eastern meditation—which many in the Western world have embraced—relies on emptying the mind. For the Christian, however, it's the opposite. We must instead focus and fill our mind with prayer, worship, scripture, and God himself. Because if we empty our mind, something will eventually fill it—something that shouldn't be there.

I also mentioned during the discussion that I don't take enough time to meditate on God's word, prayer, or praise. I make daily time for my friends and family. Why then do I not do the same for the Creator of the universe and the one who died to save me from my sins? Shouldn't he be first on my mind in the morning, throughout the day, and last on my mind as I search for sleep?

Apparently God isn't finished teaching me this lesson.

A few years ago, I purchased a book called "Morning and Evening: The Classic Daily Devotional" [39] by Charles Spurgeon. Based on last night's chat, I figured it's time I set at least fifteen minutes each day with God and God alone. Reading (and pondering) the morning lesson in the book would likely be a good start.

God loves symmetry and likes to poke at me to prove how well he knows me. In this case by teaching me the same lesson over and over again. I bet you can guess the subject of this morning's devotion.

---

[39] "Morning and Evening: The Classic Daily Devotional" by Charles Spurgeon, Barbour Publishing, Inc., ©2018

Yep, it's about finding God where we set him aside (or lost him). One example he gives is, "Did you lose Christ by neglecting the Scriptures? You must find Christ in the Scriptures."

He also says, "Take care, then, when you find your Master, to cling close to Him."

So here I am, reading, studying, pondering. Giving him a moment of my time so I may learn to cling to him, never again to let him go. We'll see how long it lasts...

At the very least, though, I'll know where to find God if I lose him again.

BRAIN FOOD

(March 2, 2021)

Everyone approaches Jesus a little bit differently. Some approach him with the heart, others with the head. Many of us use a combination of both, which is important. The most important part of God's law, after all, can be summed up with "Love God with all your heart, all your soul, and all your mind."

I can appreciate those who search for and find Jesus with their heart. I, however, am not one of them. I've certainly felt God's presence, and he comforts my heart whenever I need it. Yet I still seek him with my head first. I long to *know* him as much as I enjoy feeling his presence. I want him to teach me all about himself, and for him to show me all of his creation and how it works.

When I saw the book at my church called "The Case for the Real Jesus,"[40] how could I, in my insatiable intellectual curiosity, not pick it up?

This one addresses five attacks on Christ's identity:

1. The resurrection never happened.
2. Jesus never considered himself the Messiah.
3. The early church suppressed other, equally valid, and important gospels.
4. Scribes tampered with the Bible.
5. How Jesus dying on the cross for our sins is a "barbaric concept that would make God guilty of cosmic child abuse."

I'm on page fifty-three so far, and it's feeding my brain. Hence the title of this entry. Lee Strobel, like me, approaches God with logic, rational arguments and digs for concrete, verifiable evidence for Jesus.

His approach is similar to Dennis Prager, another one of my favorite biblical/religious scholars.

Strobel takes nothing on faith alone. Everything he believes—or chooses to believe—must be verifiable. Like his other books, he takes the reader along on his journey of discovery where he asks the difficult

---

[40] "The Case for the Real Jesus" by Lee Strobel, Zondervan, ©2007

questions. He also admits such a journey could end up changing all his notions of who God is. That's a hard road to travel, because few people want their beliefs—especially long-held beliefs—to be proven false.

It's often a matter of pride, that fear. Who likes to admit they're wrong or perhaps have been deceived? I know I don't.

Yet I also know, like Strobel, the truth matters more than anything (other than God himself). It does not change or become a lie simply because we choose to ignore or disbelieve it.

Do any of the above attacks against Jesus and Christianity have merit? You'll have to take that journey of discovery yourself. As of now, for me, my brain is full. It'll be hungry for more in the morning, I'm sure.

Luckily, unlike real food, brain food doesn't add literal fatty pounds to my belly.

A WALKING EYEBALL?

(March 27, 2021)

The instructor for my Wednesday Bible study could be described with one word: evangelist. Her heart and soul is filled with desire to bring others to Christ, to the point of overflowing. She sincerely loves Jesus like few I've ever seen.

I am simultaneously inspired, envious, and saddened at my own lack of the same.

Unlike her, I don't feel the same pull to evangelize to non-believers. As such, I can't help but ask why. Am I lacking in my own faith? Am I not focused enough on his voice and his word, so in the end he has no (or little) use of me?

Some of you will be rolling your eyes at me, I'm sure. Me questioning my strength and faith is nothing new, and some of you have expressed (for years) how silly I am to doubt my faith.

Let me assure you, I don't doubt my faith. My questions derive from my need to strengthen it. How can I do that if I don't ask questions and seek out where I'm weak?

So back to my question. Am I lacking in something, because I have neither the gift nor desire to win lost souls to Jesus?

Or do I have neither, because Jesus has other plans for me?

One thing I love about both Jesus and Paul are their surgically sharp use of exaggeration and rhetoric to make a point.

In this case, how Paul describes the Body of Christ in 1 Corinthians 12:12-31. Because of its imagery, verse 17 (ESV) in particular has always stuck with me:

"If the whole body were an eye, where would be the sense of hearing? If the whole body were an ear, where would be the sense of smell?"

The first part makes me think of Mike Wazowski in Pixar's "Monsters, Inc."[41]

Silly imagery aside, the allusion is the perfect vehicle to make a point, or as Rush Limbaugh used to say, "Being absurd to illustrate absurdity."

Paul was illustrating the absurd notion that all our gifts should be the same.

Thus proving my own absurdity for believing I and my gifts are lacking simply because my life, gifts, and desires don't mirror others.

So what then are my gifts? What does Jesus intend for me to do if it's not to evangelize to the lost?

I have to ask myself a question: What am I most passionate about, spiritually?

In the simplest terms, biblical accuracy. What I hate most is when people (Christians especially) twist scripture to mean the exact opposite of what it says. Or when they ignore certain passages in favor of others in order to give themselves license to act a certain, and often sinful way.

That's not to say I *shouldn't* point the lost to Jesus. Quite the contrary. That is the ultimate goal of all within the Body of Christ—of which I'm a part. Evangelism simply isn't my main goal. Perhaps my job instead is to encourage and help those who are.

Does my passion make me an apologist instead, perhaps even a critic?

I'll be the first to tell you, I don't know ten percent of what I should about scripture. I know just enough to be dangerous. Yet lately I've been in a studious mood both with the Bible study and reading non-fiction by those far more knowledgeable than me.

Or maybe I'm not an apologist so much, at least not yet, as I am a student. Either way, that's where I belong in the Body as of now, because that could always change.

Who am I to argue with God that I'm an ear instead of an eye—figuratively speaking?

---

41 "Monsters, Inc." Pixar Animation Studios. ©2001

AN IMPERFECT GOD?

(June 21, 2021)

I recently read a short discussion on Twitter, and it went like this:

"The God of the bible is not the same as the god of the Quran."

"god mentioned in the bible depicts him to be imperfect, while The God depicted in the Quran is absolutely perfect."

"Imperfect how? And where?"

"For starters, 1 Samuel 15:11."

Of course I had to look it up (ESV):

"I regret that I have made Saul king, for he has turned back from following me and has not performed my commandments."

Does this suggest that God expressing regret over something he did, it means he's admitting to making a mistake and is therefore imperfect? That's certainly what the Twitterite above is implying.

But is he correct?

We must first go to what "regret" means:

According to Mirriam-Webster, regret (verb) is defined as: 1(a): to mourn the loss or death of; 1(b): to miss very much; 2: to be very sorry for.

The question is, how is "regret" defined in the above passage? Was God expressing sorrow (first definition) over Saul's faithlessness, or stating he had made a mistake (2nd definition)?

Let's turn to the Hebrew term: נָחַם pronounced naw-kham'.

Strong's and NAS Exhaustive Concordance define it as "to be sorry, console oneself."

Brown-Driver-Briggs goes even deeper. It defines each Hebrew word per passage in the Old Testament. For 1 Samuel 15:11, regret is defined as "to be sorry, rue, suffer grief, repent of one's own doings."[42]

If we are to trust the last one, God is indeed sorry for or repentant of appointing Saul king—admitting he'd made a mistake.

---

[42] All concordance citations taken from Biblehub.com

Now that we're back to square one, I ask again: is God expressing regret, admitting he's imperfect? Is it truly impossible for a perfect God to have regrets? Or is that assumption incorrect?

I've heard people say, "Scripture interprets scripture." If we find a contradiction, such as 1 Samuel stating that God is admitting imperfection, whereas other verses show God to be perfect (such as in 2 Samuel 22:31 & Matthew 5:48), we must look deeper.

The first step is to read the entire chapter to discover the circumstances as well as its context and audience.

In this case, the answer over the definition of "regret" is made clearer in 1 Samuel 5:29:

"And also the Glory of Israel will not lie or have regret, for he is not a man, that he should have regret."

That says to me that God is expressing sorrow over Saul defying his word, not admitting to a mistake derived from imperfection.

What do you think?

JESUS, COME SOON?

(October 17, 2021)

The more our society collapses and evil grows ever more prevalent, the more I hear people pray the above.

Yet when their prayer seemingly continues to go unanswered (or at least a "Not yet"), they ask, "Why not? How much more does evil need to grow, to fester, and destroy? How many more people need to suffer and die under it? When will you, God, say 'enough is enough'?"

It's a prayer I refuse to utter. Would I like him to? Sure! Yet, for me, saying that prayer would come from a place of fear, laziness, and selfishness. His return would mean I no longer have to struggle, face uncertainty, and prepare for hard times which may or may not come to fruition during my lifetime.

There is another reason that has nothing and everything to do with me. Jesus is waiting in order to give people more opportunities to find him. I didn't find Jesus myself until I was sixteen. If he had decided to come earlier, I would have been denied that opportunity. Who am I to say those still lost should remain lost, because I am tired of fighting and tired of watching evil spread?

So, yes, I want Jesus to tarry a few more days. I want others to have more time and opportunity to find him—just like I did—and as such avoid the tribulations, the horrors, and the judgement that is to come.

"But do not overlook this one fact, beloved, that with the Lord one day is as a thousand years, and a thousand years as one day. The Lord is not slow to fulfill his promise as some count slowness, but is patient toward you, not wishing that any should perish, but that all should reach repentance."

~ 2 Peter 3:8-9 (ESV)

LESSONS OF CAIN

(September 26, 2022)

When asked the main lesson of Cain and Abel in Genesis—specifically why God accepted Abel's offering yet rejected Cain's—most will tell you it's because Abel's heart was in the right place. Unlike Cain's.

God even told Cain why his offering was rejected:

"Surely if you do right [t]here is uplift. But if you do not do right, sin crouches at the door; its urge is toward you. Yet you can be its master."

~ Genesis 4:7 (JSP)

I mentioned this in the comment section of an article called "What the Bible Really Says About Tithing."[43] Someone then responded that Cain's offering was rejected because it was a "fruit of the soil" offering, and not an animal. This person reasoned that blood sacrifices are found all throughout scripture as a way to point to Jesus, the Messiah, as the ultimate and final blood sacrifice for our sins.

I don't disagree about the importance of blood sacrifice for the forgiveness of sins, and how they do indeed point to Jesus. I do disagree, however, that Cain's offering was rejected due to it not being an animal.

The passage itself states why in Genesis 4:2a-4a:

"... Abel became a keeper of sheep, and Cain became a tiller of the soil. In the course of time, Cain brought an offering to the Lord from the fruit of the soil, and Abel, for his part, brought the choicest of the firstlings of his flock."

---

[43] https://www.dailywire.com/news/what-the-bible-really-says-about-tithing (another subscriber-only article)

Notice the difference in how the offerings were described. Cain merely brought a portion whereas Abel gave the choicest of his firstlings.

Many other scriptural passages describe plant/grain offerings:

"You shall also give him the first fruits of your new grain and wine and oil, and the first sheering of your sheep."

~ Deuteronomy 18:4

"You shall take some of every first fruit of the soil, which you harvest from the land that the Lord your God is giving you…"

~ Deuteronomy 26:2

"Wherefore I now bring the first fruits of the soil which You, O Lord, have given me."

~ Deuteronomy 26:10

Leviticus also included the acceptance of grain sacrifices as long as they were "first fruits" such as in Leviticus 2:14.

Not all offerings or sacrifices must be of the animal variety. That would be patently unfair (in my opinion), because not everyone did, or could, raise animals.

Back to Cain. The fact he didn't offer his first fruits was the first indication his heart was bent toward sin. He either didn't love or fear God enough or didn't think God would notice. Or both. Either way, his offering showed selfishness and contempt. No wonder God rejected it.

Cain killing Abel later was merely the end result of what had already poisoned his heart.

Still, regardless of how one reads the passage, the overall lesson is clear: before we give either to God or to others, our heart must be in the right place—To give gladly and not begrudgingly, otherwise what we give is both useless and meaningless.

NONE THE LESS

(October 9, 2022)

Nonetheless is defined as: nevertheless, however, or despite anything to the contrary.

A rather innocuous word, even if necessary, depending on the context of what's being said.

I saw a video in church today about a missionary doctor, and how God chose him to literally save lives in poverty-stricken areas of Africa. The overall message of the video was how God doesn't call the qualified; he qualifies the called.

I couldn't help but wonder at what God is calling me to do. I admit feeling a bit envious—that whatever it is, I'm not saving literal lives. Heck, I don't know if anything I do has any effect to God's kingdom, positive or negative.

Then the word "nonetheless" popped into my head, but with a few extra spaces: none the less.

God does not have a hierarchy of endowments or gifts.

As 1 Corinthians 12:4-6 (ESV) states:

"There are different kinds of gifts, but the same Spirit distributes them. There are different kinds of service, but the same Lord. There are different kinds of working, but in all of them and in everyone it is the same God at work."

The gifts God gives us are for two purposes: to glorify God and to bring others to him.

No gift is considered less important than another. My gifts may not wow anyone, and I may never know what impact they might have. Perhaps it's better that way considering I tend to be prideful. Should I know the extent of my influence, I may try to grab that glory for myself instead of pointing to God.

God is the one who gives us those gifts in the first place. We can do nothing without him (John 15:5).

Nonetheless. None the less. I doubt I'll ever see that word in the same way again.

NO RESPECTER OF PERSONS

(November 21, 2022)

The phrase above comes from Romans 2:11 (KJV):

"For there is no respect of persons with God."

Or as other translations state: God shows no partiality.

The subject in question with that verse is about a person's good works, and how God doesn't care about anyone's heritage (verse 10, ESV):

"but glory and honor and peace for everyone who does good, the Jew first and also the Greek."

Everyone has their bad days. We all face circumstances that test our resolve, our faith, our joy. Sometimes they're bad enough we're tempted to give in to despair. Most of the time, though, we endure. Sometimes we might even thrive in the end with lessons learned and wisdom gained.

Yet, at least in western cultures, we are sometimes made to feel guilty or ashamed when we cry out to God over the challenges we face.

Myself included. After all, how can any problem in my life compare to someone facing starvation, persecution, oppression, debilitating disease, abuse, slavery, etc.? How can I expect God to not scoff at me, or at least roll his eyes at my ultimately meaningless tears of frustration?

Isaiah 40:28-31 (ESV) says:

"Have you not known? Have you not heard? The Lord is the everlasting God, the Creator of the ends of the earth. He does not faint or grow weary; his understanding is unsearchable. He gives power to the faint, and to him who has no might he increases strength. Even youths shall faint and be weary, and young men shall fall exhausted; but they who wait for the LORD shall renew their strength; they shall mount up with

wings like eagles; they shall run and not be weary; they shall walk and not faint."

God not only doesn't care about my or anyone else's lineage, he doesn't hear and answer only the prayers of those with life-or-death problems. His understanding is unsearchable (or immeasurable according to other translations), so he can—and promised to—give strength to those who need it.

The Isaiah scripture above is another instance where what's not said is as important as what is said. Nowhere in the scripture above does it state the problems have to be big in order for God to strengthen us.

That said, he might convict us when we cry to him about the little things or make certain wrong assumptions about him and our circumstances. But that doesn't mean he can't understand or have compassion for our struggles. In fact, those convictions can give us the strength to move past our smaller problems a whole lot quicker.

We should never be ashamed or hesitate to cry out to God. He already knows, and we can't lie to him anyway. He never wants to see us despair, grow weary, or give in no matter who we are or how big— or how small—our problems might be.

BETRAYED BY GOD?

(January 16, 2023)

Such a thing can't be possible. Heck, some might think the very thought would be blasphemous. God can never betray anyone. It's not in his nature.

Then again, how does one define betrayal? Is it when we expect God to do what we want him to do, and he instead does the exact opposite?

In my previous entry titled "A Slap Upside the Head,"[44] I described the professional complaint against me. What I didn't get into was the time in between and the ensuing spiritual conflict. In fact, I wrestled with God quite a bit about it.

Prior to the commission meeting and being anxious about speaking before the commissioners, I had prayed God would give me peace of mind and the words I needed to say.

When I was done, and even during, I did feel confident, and several commented later about how well I did.

Why, then, did those words I thought God gave me end up being used against me? Why did God not only say no to the prayer, but allow it to be almost a complete failure, the consequences being a permanent mark on my professional record? What did God expect to achieve?

Is it not at least understandable that I would feel a bit betrayed?

Even as I struggled with God, I also struggled with myself. I knew in my head that God did not betray me. I knew he had a greater purpose than to let me be convicted by my own words.

I also knew I simply didn't understand.

Far be it for me to compare myself to any of the biblical greats, but I did feel a bit like David when he penned Psalm 22:1-2 (ESV):

"My God, my God, why have you forsaken me? Why are you so far from saving me, from the words of my groaning? [M]y God, I cry by day, but you do not answer, and by night, but I find no rest."

---

44 See entry titled "A Slap Upside the Head," page 25

I reminded myself to keep reading, so I continued with verse 3:

"Yet you are holy, enthroned on the praises of Israel."

Also in Psalm 22 is this little nugget (verse 19):

*"But you, O LORD, do not be far off! O you my help, come quickly
to my aid!"*

Once I agreed to the reprimand and the ethics class requirement, I was invited to the state board of registration meeting where they would vote on the order. I prayed for two things: For God to either give me the right words or to shut my mouth during the meeting.

Also attending was the complainant and two others. They were given an opportunity to speak to the board's decision. They each stood up and basically read me the riot act. The details are irrelevant because of what God did during the meeting.

One of the board members asked if I wanted to respond to their comments, and I merely shook my head (God had indeed shut my mouth).

I also felt an invisible wall between me and the three men as they went after my character. Not only did I not say anything, their words had absolutely no emotional impact on me. I simply looked them in the eye and listened. I knew that wall was God coming to my aid, to make sure I didn't take their words personally, and to not let this episode destroy my confidence.

In the end, even as grateful as I am, I still don't completely understand why God allowed everything to happen the way it did. Nevertheless, I learned a valuable lesson: to always be aware of my words and to be as clear as I can so there's no misinterpretation or inferences.

I'm sure I'll fail again, but hopefully not because I took for granted everyone will know exactly what I mean without being clear enough.

Regardless, God didn't betray me. Quite the contrary. He merely gave me a little bit of rope, and I took it and hanged myself with it. That's not his fault or his responsibility.

He also stood by me the entire time. I just didn't (refused to) notice until afterward.

NATURE VS GOD

(April 16, 2023)

I said in a previous entry[45] that nature no more disproves God than the artwork on the Sistine Chapel ceiling disproves Michelangelo.

A few days ago, I engaged in a friendly online debate with an atheist. He (yes, I'm assuming his gender) started with asking for proof of God. Part of the discussion is as follows:

Me: *A lack of evidence doesn't automatically negate something's existence. It could mean you merely haven't discovered that evidence, yet. My overall point is, only by searching for something will you find out for certain if it does or doesn't exist. By not looking for God and believing beyond all doubt he can't exist, of course you're not going to find him.*

Atheist: *And the converse is still true. Just because you say there is a God doesn't mean there is one.*

Me: *All the more reason to keep an open mind for the possibility, because if indeed true, the consequences of disbelief have eternal consequences.*

Atheist: *If the only motivator is fear, I want to have even less to do with it. And what if I am right how much of everyone's life is getting wasted on something that doesn't have any meaning?*

Me: *First, it's not about fear so much, but about prudence and respect. For instance, I don't fear fire, but due to my respect for its power, I prudently avoid sticking my hand in it.*

As for whether or not I discover at my death God doesn't exist, my life hasn't been wasted. Not by a long shot. God gives me peace and joy. I don't have to fear anything, not even death. Due to my faith, I can look forward to eternal life. Plus, faith in him encourages me to live righteously, lovingly, and generously, much more so than if I didn't have faith in him.

The atheist also said: *If you cannot prove that something exists, I have no interest in it. It is just who I am. I was born the scientist.*

The last comment made me think of Romans 1:19-22 (ESV):

For what can be known about God is plain to them, because God has shown it to them. For his invisible attributes, namely, his eternal power and divine nature, have been clearly perceived, ever since the creation of the world, in the things that have been made. So they are without

---

[45] "How Old Is The Universe," page 53

excuse. For although they knew God, they did not honor him as God or give thanks to him, but they became futile in their thinking, and their foolish hearts were darkened. Claiming to be wise, they became fools,

I want to concentrate on two things the atheist said: "It is who I am. I was born the scientist" and "If the only motivator is fear, I want to have less to do with it."

Romans 1:20 addresses both the scientist in this person as well as fear being a motivator (although it's not—or at least shouldn't be—the only motivator).

How?

Let's look at nature and how it shows not only God's care, but his power. And yes, we should indeed fear it (or at least be prudent when experiencing its power).

Most everyone can readily see God's care. Jesus spoke of it himself in Matthew 6:26 & 28-29:

Look at the birds of the air: they neither sow nor reap nor gather into barns, and yet your heavenly Father feeds them. Are you not of more value than they? ... And why do you worry about clothes? Consider how the lilies of the field grow: They do not labor or spin. Yet I tell you that not even Solomon in all his glory was adorned like one of these.

A few years ago, I took a picture of the night sky in the North Dakota Badlands. It shows the Milky Way, countless other stars, and Jupiter. I can't look at it and not be awed by it. God's care and beauty is evident every single star and planet. The Moon and stars shine light in the dark and show the passage of time. Plus, the most famous star, Polaris, shows us true north. It gives us direction even in the most hostile and desolate environments, and has for millennia.

Yet anyone who's lived for any amount of time knows the dangers of nature's power. Those who live on the coasts learn about the power of hurricanes. Those who live on the plains need to prepare for the occasional tornado. Those who live near a fault line should watch for earthquakes. Mountain-dwellers should tread lightly over snow lest an avalanche sweep them away. Volcanos make islands and mountains, but they also cause devastation with spewing hot lava and pyroclastic flows of rock and ash.

God is even more dangerous if we don't give him the respect, the awe, and yes, the fear he deserves.

The consequences of not taking nature or God seriously—as I said in my comments to the atheist—are eternal.

Whether or not my words made a difference, I leave that to the Holy Spirit. Although I do pray they took root, because I would like to meet this hopefully once-but-no-longer-atheist in Heaven someday.

AND LASTLY

FOR HISTORY'S SAKE, WRITE YOUR LIFE

Following are actually two entries. The first is an earlier one I happened to stumble upon recently, and it touched upon the same subject as the one titled above. I leave these for last in the hopes of encouraging you that your life matters and is worthy of being remembered.

(June 14, 2006)

My husband's grandmother wrote a series of books for her children and grandchildren. Her first book begins, in part, with this:

"Carol [her daughter] gave me a blank book entitled, 'Mom, Share Your Life With Me,' and shortly after I received another from Janeen [her granddaughter] called, 'Grandma, Tell Me Your Memories.'

"Well, I guess it's "Share and Tell" time, so here goes…

"… Remember Aesop's fable about the blind men who examined an elephant and each came up with an entirely different description? I'm sure that's the way my yarns will be received, too. Everyone remembers these episodes in their own way, but this collection is strictly from my point of view.

"My advice to you is to write down the details of unusual or important moments and file them away for the time your grandchildren ask about your life. Then your stories will be accurate instead of vague memories."

As we go through life, as we live it, we don't normally see the historical importance, not just to succeeding generations, but to all who come after. History books rarely convey the beauty, the horror, the raw emotions of living through great and terrible events. Children are left with mere when, why, and how things happened. They read or hear the facts without the experiences, and the chances of those events "sticking" with them are lessened.

I am one of those who doesn't see the significance of my life for the future. What possible contributions can I make now, in my mere thirty-six years of life to future generations?

Except that's really not the point. When the past needs to be remembered for others, will I recall vividly what happened, or vaguely?

Taking a quick look back, I still have vivid recollections of the Challenger shuttle explosion, when President Reagan was shot, Desert Storm, 9/11, the fall of Bagdad, Hurricanes Rita and Katrina. And those are just off the top of my head. Will I remember those events twenty or even fifty years from now if I live that long? Not likely. What also about my family who simply want to know me, how my husband and I lived our lives? Will I bring forth those cherished memories well enough others will cherish them as well?

If I am to die tomorrow, what of my life will I have left behind as far as my memories and experiences? Not much.

So why not start writing down the events in my life, both small and great for untold futures to enjoy and learn from?

(August 19, 2017)

In today's society the loudest people get all the attention. Biases in news agencies grow more obvious and prevalent. Because of that, those not in the literal midst of important events have a difficult time understanding what's true and what's false.

I don't recommend we ignore important events, but I do recommend we do our research and see if we can find people who lived it and get their perspective. We should also seek out more than one person, and from multiple sides. Only then will the truth eventually be found.

Discernment is key. And honesty.

I read a writer's devotional[46] yesterday focused on Aleksandr Solzhenitsyn (1918-2008) who "wrote books that shed a true light on what was happening behind the Iron Curtain."

Without him and others who wrote and spoke fearlessly and honestly about what happened in their country, the truth of that time may have never been revealed.

---

[46] "The Writer's Devotional: 165 Inspirational Exercises, Ideas, Tips & Motivations on Writing" by Amy Peters, Sterling Publishing, ©2012, page 14

We must do the same.

With all the furor over so-called offensive statues from the Civil War and calls to rename everything because some people find it offensive is not only silly, but dangerous. As ugly as our history is at times (and no country can claim otherwise), destroying it is uglier. If we're not honest and open about our history, we can never learn and grow from it.

And where does it end? Will we now destroy the writings of people who lived during that time, because what they wrote offends some people?

Who ultimately gets to decide what's offensive anyway?

Plenty of people find the U.S. founding documents offensive—including the Constitution—simply because it was written by people who did what many now consider unconscionable. Yet who wrote them is unimportant compared to the documents themselves. Should we ignore the wisdom of Dr. Martin Luther King, Jr. because he cheated on his wife?

But I get off topic.

We live in interesting times, sometimes dangerous times. If we don't chronicle them and do so with complete honesty, our children will never know what we accomplished—both good and bad—and they will, in effect, never learn from either. History will then be guaranteed to repeat itself.

It might anyway, but that's another subject.

"I believe that world literature has it in its power to help mankind, in these its troubled hours, to see itself as it really is, notwithstanding the indoctrinations of prejudiced people, and parties."

~ Aleksandr Solzhenitsyn